The Mystery of the Church

HIPPOBOOKS

Fabrice Katembo is determined to follow the biblical truth wherever it will lead him. In this study of the New Testament church and its relation to the church in Africa, he labors well to write in a biblically clear way. Fabrice has a refreshing burden for biblically healthy African churches, and in his analysis he accurately surveys not only the Scriptures but relevant African theologians. Here is an author worthy of your time. *Tolle Lege!* (Take up and read!)

Daniel Huffstutler, ThM
Pastor,
Redeemer Bible Church, Nairobi, Kenya

Fabrice Katembo has explained the mystery of the church of Christ in very captivating, simple, and clear terms, unlike many other scholars who complicate the truth of God's word in the name of prowess in higher theological scholarship. In the final two chapters, although he differs markedly with other renowned African theologians such as John S. Mbiti and Kwame Bediako (such as on whether the true God of Israel is the Supreme Being in African traditional religions and other aspects), Katembo has endeavoured as best as he can to present the implications of the revealed mystery of the church on the African context. Readers may not agree with all that he has written, but it is an outstanding book worth reading and interacting with from beginning to end.

Nathan Nzyoka Joshua, PhD
Lecturer in Biblical Studies,
Africa International University (NEGST), Nairobi, Kenya

This book helpfully provides readers an overview of Paul and his theology before examining the concept of the church as a "mystery." As Katembo notes, churches in Africa often struggle with divisions. Thus, this work provides a way for Christians to think about what it means to be the church. The book is accessible while providing both scholarly support for the author's claims and taking the church's context into account.

Stephanie M. Lowery, PhD
Lecturer in Theological Studies,
Africa International University (NEGST), Nairobi, Kenya

I offer high praise for Fabrice S. Katembo's latest work, *The Mystery of the Church*. With a spirit that is reminiscent of the late Byang Kato, Katembo takes an unashamed biblical perspective on ecclesiology and applies it to modern

Africa. In this work, Katembo brings to light the theological weaknesses of a few of the earliest and most respected African theologians like Mbiti, Bediako, and Idowu. While applauding their attempts to find connections between Christianity and African Traditional Religion, he demonstrates that some of their conclusions do not stand up to the witness of Scripture. Katembo is one of the new generation of African theologians who are academically gifted and respectful of the past, but thoroughly committed to the truth of Scripture above culture or tradition. His work is a breath of fresh air and an exciting application of ancient truth to modern life.

Kevin W. Rodgers, PhD
Africa Baptist Theological Education Network

This book provides an apt, accessible, and clear exposition of Paul's understanding of the mystery of the church with particular application to contemporary African Christianity. Avoiding technical language, the book covers Paul's life and theology, metaphors of the church, African traditional religions, the Christologies of three prominent African theologians, and the church as the body of Christ. What I find most helpful about this book is its simplicity and bravery. It is written with pastoral concern for a wide readership. Thus, lay Christians, preachers, and students will find it valuable.

David Kirwa Tarus, PhD
Executive Director,
Association for Christian Theological Education in Africa (ACTEA)

Fabrice Katembo has provided us with a good overview of Paul's theology of the church, with a unique focus on its implications for the church in Africa. Taking up the mantle of Byang Kato, he rightly subjects African traditional religions to the authority of the Word of God, rejecting syncretism. He appropriately upholds the gospel as the solution to ethnic division. Katembo's work is saturated throughout with Scripture; it is gospel-centred, and Christ-exalting.

Jamie Viands, PhD
Lecturer in Biblical Studies,
Africa International University (NEGST), Nairobi, Kenya

The Mystery of the Church

Applying Paul's Ecclesiology in Africa

Fabrice S. Katembo

HIPPOBOOKS

© 2020 Fabrice S. Katembo

Published 2020 by HippoBooks, an imprint of ACTS and Langham Publishing.
Africa Christian Textbooks (ACTS), TCNN, PMB 2020, Bukuru 930008, Plateau State, Nigeria.
www.actsnigeria.org

Langham Publishing, PO Box 296, Carlisle, Cumbria CA3 9WZ, UK
www.langham.org

ISBNs:
978-1-83973-056-6 Print
978-1-83973-086-3 ePub
978-1-83973-087-0 Mobi
978-1-83973-088-7 PDF

British Library Cataloguing-in-Publication Data
A catalogue record for this book is available from the British Library

ISBN: 978-1-83973-056-6

Cover & Book Design: projectluz.com

Contents

Introduction

When I talk of applying Paul's ecclesiology, I do not intend to do an assessment or a careful evaluation of literary works on the church. This study is an attempt to understand the mystery of the church as explained by Paul in his epistles. It is not my intent to critically review and debate all scholarly works on the subject matter, but the purpose of this study is to lead the reader "from a position outside the Bible to one inside it,"[1] for a better understanding of Paul's concept of the mystery of the church. Thus, this study is limited to a framework of Pauline epistles.

There are excellent books on understanding the mystery of the church, for example G. K. Beale and Benjamin L. Gladd, *Hidden but Now Revealed: A Biblical Theology of Mystery*; John S. Feinberb, *Continuity and Discontinuity: Perspectives on the Relationship between the Old and New Testaments*; Oswald T. Allis, *Prophecy and the Church*, etc. While these books entail a broad study and a more technical approach to the mystery, this book is intended to help the reader understand the mystery of the church based on the writings of the apostle Paul. My purpose is to introduce the reader into the discussion rather than doing a critical analysis of different scholastic views.

Lots of scholarship on the mystery of the church pursue both a theological and exegetical approach but without bridging the application to our world today. Thus in my approach, I seek to understand the mystery of the church considering African Christianity. For instance, it could be argued there is continuity on the understanding of God between African traditional religions and Christianity. But it is my opinion that we cannot defend the validity of African traditional religions considering only the Old Testament. We must look at it through the lenses of New Testament truth as well. A clear Pauline description of the gentiles will reveal that in trying to trace this continuity is a terrible temptation to sideline the gospel truth about the person and work of Christ.

---

1. Eugene Merrill, Mark F. Rooker, and Michael A. Grisanti, *The World and the Word: An Introduction to the Old Testament* (Nashville: B&H, 2011), 1.

What Is the Mystery of the Church?

There has been a tremendous division of the church in Africa. Our generation seems to be gradually branded by divisions of tribalism, political parties, racism, ethnic conflicts, church denominations, etc. There are still increasing indications of an awareness that the problems are more alarming than we realize. Sadly, most of us are the greatest problems the church in Africa has ever faced which is clear evidence that the gospel has not yet sunk deeply into the core of our hearts. A failure to understand the riches of grace we all share in Christ will result in a disaster that we will fail to resolve. Consequently, there is urgency in Africa about understanding the mystery of the church.

What is a mystery? The first entry of the Oxford dictionary defines "mystery" as something that is difficult to understand, to explain, or to prove scientifically. According to Allis, the word "mystery" "occurs 29 times in the New Testament, most of which are in Paul's epistles, 6 being in Ephesians."[2] In the Bible, especially in the New Testament, this word carries a more interesting meaning. The Greek word for mystery in the New Testament, *mustêrion*, has a connotation of something formerly unknown but now revealed, something hidden or a secret which has been now revealed. Allis states that, "according to Paul, a mystery may be a truth which can only be understood by believers or a truth only partly known to them, but not necessarily something entirely new or utterly unknown."[3]

No other Scripture in the Bible gives us a more concrete definition than Ephesians 3:4–5. According to Paul, a mystery is something that has been hidden in the Old Testament but now revealed in the New Testament. Beale and Gladd define this mystery as "the revelation of God's partially hidden wisdom, particularly as it concerns events occurring in the 'latter days.'"[4] What is this secret that the past generations could not know completely? What is this that the Old Testament saints were not able to grasp fully?

As we will discover later in this book, the people of past generations could not see that the church would come into existence where both Jews and gentiles would be fellow heirs of the heavenly blessings in the body of Christ – the reconciliation of Jews and gentiles into one body. The Old Testament saints did not see the church's "present mixed character versus its future consummation

---

2. Oswald T. Allis, *Prophecy and the Church* (Phillipsburg, NJ: Presbyterian and Reformed Publishing, 1974), 90.

3. Allis, *Prophecy and the Church*, 90–91.

4. G. K. Beale and Benjamin L. Gladd, *Hidden but Now Revealed: A Biblical Theology of Mystery* (Downers Grove, IL: InterVarsity Press, 2014), 20.

in beauty and purity."[5] In the following pages, we will spend our time trying to understand this mystery of the church and its impact in Africa.

The Shape of This Book

I have divided this book in two parts. In the first part, I will explain briefly the life of Paul and his ecclesiology. In the second part, I will expand on the idea of our union with Christ and its consequences in Africa. As we move into the last two chapters, you might notice a great shift of tone. In the first three chapters, I want us to understand the theology of the church. What is the church? Why does the church exist? Who are in the church? etc. In the last two chapters, we will move into Africa in order to figure out how what we have learned applies to the church in Africa. We will also try to see how African Christianity fits in the theme of the mystery of the church.

I begin in chapter 1 with the life and theology of Paul, but this is not an exhaustive account of Paul's ministry. There are thousands of books on the life and ministry of Paul. Although I do not intend to provide a full account of his life, I briefly address here Paul's education, his citizenship, his conversion, his call to preach to the gentiles, and his apostleship. In this chapter, I also briefly introduce a systematic overview of Pauline theology.

The vast part of the information about Paul's life and ministry will come from the book of Acts and his own autobiographical testimonies (Rom 11:1; 1 Cor 15:9; 2 Cor 11:22; Gal 1:13–17; Phil 3:4–6). As we shall see later, Paul's speech at his arrest in Jerusalem gives us a summary of who he was, "I am a Jew, born in Tarsus in Cilicia, but brought up in this city, educated at the feet of Gamaliel according to the strict manner of the law of our fathers, being zealous for God as all of you are this day" (Acts 22:3).

Chapter 2 focuses on the different metaphors Paul uses to illustrate the mystery of the church. We will examine a number of Scriptures that describe the church as one living organism. As we will see, each metaphor carries with it an idea that describes the relationship between Christ and the church. Paul uses different figures to emphasize his argument of how the wall of hostility that used to separate the Jews and the gentiles has been abolished in Christ.

For example, Paul represents the church as a building where Christ is the cornerstone (Eph 2:21–20; see also 1 Cor 3:11). We will also see how the church is represented as the bride of Christ. This image emphasizes how the people

---

5. William Hendriksen, *The Gospel of Matthew: New Testament Commentary* (Edinburgh: Banner of Truth, 1973), 553.

of God are regarded as the wife and Christ as the husband where the church appropriately submits to Christ, her head (Eph 5:22–24). We will also look at other metaphors: the church as the body of Christ, the church as the temple, and the church as the flock of God.

In chapter 3, given the different figures of the church, it will therefore be appropriate to exegete one of the great themes of Paul – the mystery of the church. It is my conviction that in order to understand Paul's thinking on the mystery, a very careful study is appropriate. Therefore to do the task, I have selected Ephesians 3:1–10 as the text that will best explain the mystery of the church. As I will discuss in this chapter, Paul describes the gentiles as "separated from Christ, alienated from the commonwealth of Israel and strangers to the covenants of promise, having no hope and without God in the world" (Eph 2:12). But Paul then shows how all these things about the gentiles have changed; they "are no longer strangers and aliens, but you are fellow citizens with the saints and members of the household of God" (2:19).

Once a basic familiarity with the mystery is achieved, in chapter 4 my focus will shift to African traditional religions. In this chapter, I will briefly emphasize the concept of the person and work of Christ in Africa. In order to frame the issue, I will refer to Kwame Bediako, E. B. Idowu and John Mbiti a lot simply because they are very well-known and very interesting, but also because they put a lot of thought into the issue of continuity and discontinuity of the understanding of God that is still the focus of lively debates. In many ways, their writings referred in this book are presenting some of the ideas that I think we can engage with very properly. For instance, they have argued that since there are some similarities between African traditional religions and the Jewish religion, there must be a certain continuity of the understanding of God. In other words, since Africans have been worshipers of God in the pre-Christian era, the introduction of Christianity only came to mark the continuity of the understanding of God in Africa. But it is my conviction that since God first established a covenant with the people of Israel (Exod 19:5–6; Deut 4:9–10), the mystery must be understood in terms of Jews and gentiles (non-Jews) and not in terms of African gentiles versus non-African gentiles. In other words, the mystery is about the coming of the Jews and the gentiles into one organism: the church. Since the church includes Jewish believers and African believers, who are part of the gentile people, this chapter seeks to understand the mystery of the church in light of African traditional religions.

In chapter 5, I will dwell more on Paul's portrayal of the church as the body of Christ. If the church is the body of Christ, of which he is the head, this metaphor conveys the reality that believers are one body, however, distinct.

Thus, believers have a mutual cooperation; they are indivisible because of their reconciliation with God in Christ. How does this idea of the believers' union with Christ help in solving the key issues that Africa faces, such as ethnic conflicts, tribalism, racism, etc.? Since Africans are part of the mystery, how does this truth contribute to our social interpretation of traditions, for example intertribal marriages? What can we learn about African traditional practices and beliefs in light of the believers' union with Christ?

It is not my intention in this chapter to expand on the subject of ecumenism in Africa. This chapter is about the unity within the church and not the unity of churches. Frankly, there is a need to address the issue of ecumenism in Africa since, in the words of Byang Kato, "the ecumenical ship with its imported contraband of liberal theology is making its presence felt."[6] Also, the differences of church denominations hold the potential for creating a disdain among themselves, and therefore treating one another as unworthy. However, I will not follow through that point simply because it's an area that deals with the theological or the doctrinal unity of the church. My focus is mainly on the unity within the church as a solution to ethnic conflicts in Africa.

Finally, I hope that this volume will help readers with information necessary to better understand the church. I have attempted to make this book accessible so it will prove useful to laypeople, pastors, students, and those who engage with the Scriptures. This volume does not contain technical words, it is written in a readable style. Lastly, I am open to any suggestions that may improve this book.

---

6. Byang H. Kato, *Theological Pitfalls in Africa* (Kisumu, Kenya: Evangel, 1975), 148.

Part 1

Paul and the Theology
of the Church

1

The Life and Theology of Paul

Parallel to his writings, the book of Acts is one of the sources from which we draw much information about Paul. As we delve into this study, it is my conviction that understanding Paul is one of the prerequisites to interpreting his writings. Thus, a study of Paul is essential for our understanding of the mystery of the church.

Who is Paul? Where was he from? Did Paul study Greek rhetoric and use it in his letters? Was Paul's education formal or institutional? Why did Paul persecute the church of Christ? How was Paul converted to Christianity? What are the main themes of Paul's theology? How did Paul defend his apostleship or his call to preach to the gentiles? While attempting to answer these questions, my hope is that the effect of a study on Paul will provide information we need to understand Paul's ministry to the gentiles and his theology.

Who Is Paul?

Paul's Hebrew name was Saul. Although we know nothing about his date of birth, Paul was born in Tarsus, the capital and chief city of the Roman province of Cilicia in Asia Minor (Acts 9:11; 21:39; 22:3). Tarsus was ranked among the greatest educational centers along with Athens and Alexandria. Since the city was Hellenistic,[1] most of its residents were familiar with Greek culture including literature, philosophy, beliefs, etc. Though neither Luke nor Paul mention that Paul attended any school in Tarsus, he was familiar with Greek

---

1. The Oxford dictionary defines the adjective "Hellenistic" as something connected with Greek history, language, and culture of the fourth through the first centuries BC. In this book, I adopted the definition of Louis H. Feldman in his book *Judaism and Hellenism Reconsidered* (Boston: Brill Academic, 2006).

philosophy and "had the ability to write reasonably good Greek."[2] He probably studied it before moving to Jerusalem to sit under Gamaliel's education.

Paul's parents were Jews (Phil 3:5). In fact, Paul boldly asserts to be both a descendant of the tribe of Benjamin and the offspring of Abraham (Rom 11:1; 2 Cor 11:22). His father was a Pharisee (Acts 23:6) and a Roman citizen, hence Paul was a Roman citizen by birth (Acts 22:28; see also 16:37). We are not sure whether he had many siblings, but Luke records that Paul had a sister (Acts 23:16). Though the book of Acts and Paul's writings seem to be quiet on why Paul's parents or grandparents had moved from the Holy Land to live in the diaspora, we clearly see that his parents were devoted Jews since they sought to maintain their traditional lifestyles, or their Jewish customs in the Hellenistic environment. For example, Paul says he was circumcised on the eighth day as was Jewish custom.

Paul's family probably used to visit Jerusalem for different occasions since "Jerusalem was the religious focus of Jews throughout the world and the one to which they contributed each year and which they visited during the three pilgrimage festivals."[3] Paul's parents were sincere devotees to the Jewish religion. And since his father was a Pharisee, they doubtlessly tried to follow the Torah and the Prophets.

Education

Since Paul's father was a Pharisee, thus a devoted Jew, Paul probably benefited from his primary education in the home under his father's instruction (Exod 13:8, 14; Deut 6:20–21; 11:18–21; Prov 4:1, 10–11). The Pharisees believed both the Torah and the Prophets. So from his early age, Paul would have been exposed to the sacred texts and traditions which are reflected in his writings.

In his early youth, Paul moved from Tarsus to Jerusalem. We don't know exactly the reason for this move, but he probably moved there because Jerusalem was the place of the Jewish temple and the seat of Judaic education. In Jerusalem, Paul was thoroughly taught Jewish theology under the feet of the Pharisee Gamaliel (Acts 22:3). Gamaliel had a great influence in Jewish education and was a man of permanent renown among the Jews (Acts 5:34–40). According to F. F. Bruce, Gamaliel was "a pharisaic leader of quite exceptional

---

2. Graham N. Stanton and Guy G. Stroumsa, eds., *Tolerance and Intolerance in Early Judaism and Christianity* (Cambridge: Cambridge University Press, 1998), 114.

3. Louis H. Feldman, *Judaism and Hellenism Reconsidered* (Boston: Brill Academic, 2006), 677.

eminence and the greatest teacher of the day. . . . he was a disciple of Hillel, whom he succeeded as head of his school."[4]

Due to his home education and Gamaliel's teachings, "the primary influences on Paul's thought came from Pharisaic Judaism rather than the broader Hellenistic culture."[5] For example Paul's circumcision on the eighth day demonstrates the fact that his parents were not deeply influenced by the prevalent Hellenistic culture. In fact, if we define Hellenization as a "process of acculturation by which behavior, manners, culture (literature, philosophy, art), religious belief, ethical, social, political, economic, and material norms, etc., of a person or a group might be affected by the kind of Greek culture that spread in the lands that came under the rule of Alexander the Great,"[6] then we may conclude that Paul was not deeply influenced by Hellenism, even though Luke records Paul's debate with the Athenian philosophers (Acts 17:16–34). Luke seems to focus on both Paul the Judaic and Paul the Christian, but not on Paul the Hellenist. Paul was familiar with the Greek culture since it is my understanding that he studied in Tarsus. However, any study of Paul's writings reveals that he was endowed with remarkable moral and intellectual gifts.

Called to Preach

What was behind Paul's passion to persecute the church? Why did he become so zealous in destroying both Jewish and gentile Christians? Was he defending the law? Was it because of Jacob's words concerning the tribe of Benjamin of which Paul was a descendant, "Benjamin is a ravenous wolf, in the morning devouring the prey and at evening dividing the spoil" (Gen 49:27)?

In his epistle to the Romans, Paul argues that his fellow Jews had zeal for God but were ignorant about the righteousness of God to everyone who believes in Christ – both Jews and gentiles (Rom 10:1–4). They had misunderstood the Scriptures and thus were misguided; their zeal was "not according to knowledge." Paul claims to be a witness of this zeal for God. Like his fellow Jews, he had formerly exhibited a similar religious zeal for God deprived of the knowledge of God's righteousness "which comes through faith in Christ, the righteousness from God that depends on faith" (Phil 3:9). Thus having been

4. F. F. Bruce, *The Book of the Acts: The New International Commentary of the New Testament*, rev. ed. (Grand Rapids: Eerdmans, 1988), 114.

5. Scot McKnight and Grant R. Osborne, *The Face of New Testament Studies: A Survey of Recent Research* (Grand Rapids: Baker Academic, 2004), 306.

6. Feldman, *Judaism and Hellenism Reconsidered*, 4.

ignorant of the fact that Christ, the righteousness of God, "has broken down in his flesh the dividing wall of hostility" (Eph 2:14) between the gentiles and the Jews, Paul's zeal to protect Israel's separateness from the gentiles was the reason for his passion to persecute believing Jews – who suddenly became ignorant of the "dividing wall" – and gentiles who dirtied the holiness of Israel by their intrusion in the name of Christ. James D. G. Dunn argues that,

> Zeal was the characteristic motivation of those earlier in Israel's history who had determined to prevent any disregard for, or crossing of, the boundaries between Israel and the nations that might threaten Israel's holiness, and it was this same zeal that obviously explains the violence of Paul's persecution (Phil 3:6).[7]

In his ignorance, Paul believed with all his heart that what he was doing was right and acceptable to the God of Israel, "a combination of zeal and ignorance" in Stott's words. Stott explains that, "the proper word for zeal without knowledge, commitment without reflection, or enthusiasm without understanding, is fanaticism. And fanaticism is a horrid and dangerous state to be in."[8]

Furthermore, his explanation in Galatians 1:13–16 is sufficient to enable us to draw out the reason why Paul persecuted the church: "And I was advancing in Judaism beyond many of my own age among my people, so extremely zealous was I for the traditions of my fathers" (v. 14). Paul's progress in Pharisaic Judaism had made him such an enthusiastic persecutor that Luke describes him as "breathing threats and murder against the disciples of the Lord" (Acts 9:1). Paul was advancing in the traditions of his fathers rather than following his teacher Gamaliel, since Gamaliel at one time opposed persecution (Acts 5:34–39). William Hendriksen says,

> For Paul this incentive was supplied by the progress which he had made in Pharisaic Judaism, a religion of works and bondage, and by his recognition of the fact that this was the very opposite of the Christian religion of grace, and freedom. He thoroughly understood that Judaism and Christianity were irreconcilable enemies.[9]

---

7. McKnight and Osborne, *Face of New Testament Studies*, 342.

8. John Stott, *Romans: God's Good News for the World* (Downers Grove, IL: InterVarsity Press, 1994), 279–80.

9. William Hendriksen, *Galatians and Ephesians: New Testament Commentary* (Edinburgh: Banner of Truth, 1968), 50.

Paul the persecutor could not see the promise made to Abraham being fulfilled – the blessing of the nations through Abraham (Gen 12:1–3). But this promise is kept in Christ, in whom both the Jews and gentiles form one organism and in whom both Jews and gentiles are made right with God by grace alone through faith alone like their spiritual father, Abraham. In his pre-conversion life, Paul believed that a person is made right with God by the law and not by faith.

Initially Paul vigorously opposed and persecuted the earliest Christians. He later told Agrippa, "I punished them often in all the synagogues and tried to make them blaspheme, and in raging fury against them I persecuted them even to foreign cities" (Acts 26:11). At last, on his way to Damascus, Paul encountered the resurrected Christ who had been crucified some years back but was "now the heavenly Lord, the one whom he was zealously persecuting in the person of his followers."[10] And Paul was dramatically converted to Christ "resulting in a God-ordained mission to the Gentiles."[11] Paul became an industrious preacher who founded many churches in Asia Minor.

The very zeal that drove Paul to attempt to destroy this mystery became the same passion that drove him to proclaim it. The man who had ignorantly denied the core of Christian doctrine passionately taught that salvation is designed by God for all people, both Jews and gentiles, who put their faith in Jesus Christ, and that the burden of the law is inconsistent with the spiritual freedom which Jesus gives.

Paul's Apostleship

According to the *Tyndale Bible Dictionary*, in the New Testament, the word apostle "was used to designate those who had been sent by Jesus with the proclamation of the gospel. From among the wider group of those who followed him, Jesus selected twelve men who maintained with him a particularly close relationship, receiving private instruction and witnessing his miracles and controversy with the Jewish authorities."[12] Martyn Lloyd-Jones gives us a remarkable definition: "an apostle is one chosen and sent with a special mission

---

10. Bruce, *Book of the Acts*, 183.

11. McKnight and Osborne, *Face of New Testament Studies*, 298.

12. Philip W. Comfort and Walter A. Elwell, *The Tyndale Bible Dictionary: A Comprehensive Guide to the People, Places, and Important Words of the Bible* (Carol Stream, IL: Tyndale, 2001), 96.

as the fully authorized representative of the sender."[13] From these definitions, we may come up with some qualifications of an apostle.

An apostle is one who has seen the risen Lord. An apostle had to be a witness to the resurrection of the Lord Jesus Christ. This is clearly seen in the book of Acts when the eleven disciples of Jesus wanted to choose someone to replace Judas. And there were two criteria used: they needed a man (1) who had accompanied the disciples during the time that the Lord Jesus went in and out among them; and (2) who had been a witness to Christ's resurrection (Acts 1:21–22). You could not be an apostle without having been a witness of the resurrection of Jesus Christ.

Thus, Paul clearly asserts that the resurrection appearance of Christ on the Damascus road is what qualified him as an apostle, "Am I not free? Am I not an apostle? Have I not seen Jesus our Lord?" (1 Cor 9:1). Paul goes on to say, "For I delivered to you as of first importance what I also received: Christ died for our sins in accordance with the Scriptures, that he was buried, that he was raised on the third day in accordance with the Scriptures, and he appeared to Cephas, then to the twelve . . . Last of all, as to one untimely born, he appeared also to me" (1 Cor 15:3–5, 8). Paul consistently links these apostolic claims to a specific event in the past in which the risen Lord appeared to him (Acts 9:1–9).

An apostle is one who has been specially called to be an apostle. Before a man could be an apostle, he had to be specifically called by the Lord himself. And Paul never seems to have been in doubt that his apostleship was "to the gentiles." It will be useful to quote all the passages in which Paul asserts that his call as an apostle was to the gentiles:

> For I would have you know, brothers, that the gospel that was preached by me is not man's gospel. For I did not receive it from any man, nor was I taught it, but I received it through a revelation of Jesus. . . . [he] was pleased to reveal his Son to me, in order that I might preach him among the Gentiles, I did not immediately consult with anyone. (Gal 1:11–12, 16)

> On the contrary, when they saw that I had been entrusted with the gospel to the uncircumcised, just as Peter had been entrusted with the Gospel to the circumcised (for he who worked through Peter for his apostolic ministry to the circumcised worked also through me for mine to the Gentiles), and when James and Cephas and

---

13. Martyn Lloyd-Jones, *Romans, Exposition of Chapter 1: The Gospel of God* (Edinburgh: Banner of Truth, 1985), 38.

John, who seemed to be pillars, perceived the grace that was given to me, they gave the right hand of fellowship to Barnabas and me, that we should go to the Gentiles and they to the circumcised. (Gal 2:7–9)

Now I am speaking to you Gentiles. Inasmuch then as I am an apostle to the Gentiles, I magnify my ministry. (Rom 11:13)

Along these claims, we may conclude that the appearance of Christ to Paul on the road to Damascus marks his commission to preach to the gentiles. John Stott says,

"Apostle" was a distinctively Christian name from the beginning, in that Jesus himself chose it as his designation of the Twelve, and Paul claimed to have been added to their number. The distinctive qualifications of the apostles were that they were directly and personally called and commissioned by Jesus, that they were eyewitnesses of the historical Jesus, at least (and especially) of his resurrection, and that they were sent out by him to preach with his authority.[14]

An apostle is one who has been given authority to do certain things. One of these things is that he is given authority and a commission to work miracles. In 2 Corinthians 12:12, Paul says, "The signs of a true apostle were performed among you with utmost patience, with signs and wonders and mighty works." This verse clearly shows that the apostles were given certain gifts such as healing and performing miracles and wonders. William Hendriksen concludes with these words about the apostle Paul.

He is a sent, a commissioned one (cf. John 20:21), an apostle in the deepest, richest sense, fully clothed with the authority of the One who sent him. His apostleship is equal to that of the Twelve. Hence, we speak of "the Twelve and Paul." Elsewhere he even stresses the fact that the risen and exalted Savior had appeared to him just as truly as to Cephas (1 Cor 15:5, 8; cf. 9:1). The Savior had assigned to him a task so broad and universal that his entire life was henceforth to be occupied with it.[15]

---

14. Stott, *Romans*, 46.
15. Hendriksen, *Galatians and Ephesians*, 29–30.

An Overview of Pauline Theology

Pauline theology as reflected in the epistles we have from his pen provides a solid foundation for understanding Christian theology. Unlike other epistles, Pauline epistles cover almost a quarter of the New Testament. Along with other books of the Bible, Pauline epistles are a bedrock to understanding the doctrine of God, the person of Jesus Christ, the Holy Spirit, salvation, humanity and sin, and the last things.[16]

The Doctrine of God

When God reveals himself, he does so according to his own character and nature. In this Pauline theology, we attempt to understand the truth that God has revealed concerning himself.

The Existence of God

In Romans 1, Paul speaks of the knowledge of God that is plain and can be perceived by all people of all times through creation (Rom 1:19–20). In Romans 2, Paul also speaks about the law being written on human hearts which reflects an awareness of the existence of God, a sense of deity inbuilt in all people (Rom 2:14–16). Alister McGrath writes, "God has endowed human beings with some inbuilt sense or presentment of the divine existence. It is as if something about God has been engraved in the heart of every human being."[17] Theologians have classified these two ways of knowing God as general revelation.

The idea of general revelation raises questions: Can general revelation lead to an increased appreciation of God? Does general revelation reveal the salvific plan of God? Can a careful observation of the wonders of creation lead to faith in God? To answer these questions, Paul points out that even though creation serves as a way in which God reveals his existence, sinners have suppressed this knowledge. Since "no one seeks for God" (Rom 3:11), human beings have failed to respond to the truth about God through general revelation. Instead, they have suppressed it.

Paul asserts that God may be fully known through Jesus Christ, "the image of the invisible God, the firstborn of all creation" (Col 1:15). This knowledge

---

16. I have chosen, in this section, not to talk about Pauline ecclesiology since it is the focus of this book.

17. Alister McGrath, *Christian Theology: An Introduction*, 6th ed. (Chichester: John Wiley, 2017), 143.

of God provided to us in Scripture climaxes in the life, death, and resurrection of Jesus Christ (Rom 6:9–10; 7:4; 1 Cor 15:20; Eph 1:16–21; etc.).

The Righteousness of God

Righteousness is defined as the "fulfillment of expectations in any relationship whether with God or other people."[18] Since God is righteous (Rom 10:3), he expects righteousness from human beings who are to reflect the nature of their Creator. And if God is righteous, then God's acts cannot be in contradiction to his righteousness. God's judgment is righteous (Rom 2:5; 2 Thess 1:5–8; 2 Tim 4:8), and he judges each one according to his or her works (Rom 2:6–8). He also judges without partiality (Rom 2:11–12).

But the dilemma is that people cannot attain God's righteousness by their own efforts to keep the law; therefore, it must be a gift from God (Rom 3:20–25; 5:16–17). Thus, God declares people as righteous when they put their faith in Christ Jesus (Phil 3:9) "who was delivered up for our trespasses and raised for our justification" (Rom 4:25). Therefore, they receive forgiveness of their sins and eternal life (Col 2:13–14; 1 Tim 1:16).

God's act of declaring people righteous in Christ is termed as "justification." Justification goes hand in hand with righteousness. R. C. Sproul explains, "God transfers righteousness from the account of Christ to the account of everyone who believes. In justification, there is a double transfer. Our sin was transferred to Christ on the cross; his righteousness is transferred to us."[19]

The Sovereignty of God

The word "sovereign" suggests the idea of an absolute ruler. In his writings, Paul seems not to use this word, but he does use terms that describe the sovereignty of God in its application. Here are some examples.

Predestination: Paul describes the sovereignty of God in salvation when he states that God decreed the salvation of human beings from eternity past (Rom 8:30; 1 Cor 2:7; Eph 1:3–6; 1:11–12).

Election: Another word Paul uses to suggest the idea of God's sovereignty in salvation is the word "elect" or "election" (Rom 8:33; 9:11; 11:5, 7, 28; Col 3:12; 1 Thess 1:4–5; 2 Tim 2:10; Titus 1:1). Election is that act of God's free will by which before the foundation of the world (Eph 1:3–5) he decreed his spiritual blessings to certain or chosen people.

---

18. Comfort and Elwell, *Tyndale Bible Dictionary*, 96.

19. R. C. Sproul, *Truths We Confess: Volume Two – Salvation and the Christian Life* (Phillipsburg, NJ: P&R, 2007), 46.

The Calling of God: Paul, in Romans 8:28, says that all things work together for good to those who have been called by God. This call brings new life (Eph 2:1–5) to men and women who were once "dead in the sins and trespasses" (Eph 2:1) before God called them. In other words, they could not come to life unless God called them. This carries the idea of God being sovereign in drawing sinners to salvation. In his portrayal of "a servant of God," Paul further asserts that God can impress his will on those who oppose the truth: "Gently instruct those who oppose the truth. Perhaps God will change those people's hearts, and they will learn the truth" (2 Tim 2:25 NLT). This call is also an invitation to the hope (Eph 4:4) found in Christ Jesus through salvation. The people who are called also obtain the glory of the Lord Jesus Christ (Rom 8:30; 2 Thess 2:13–14).

Foreknowledge: This term, according to Paul, does not suggest the idea that God knew who will be saved beforehand. But it simply means that God made the sovereign choice to set his love on those who are called to "be conformed to the image of his Son" (Rom 8:29).

The Person of Jesus Christ

The Humanity of Jesus Christ

Paul presents strong arguments about the humanity of Christ. For example in Romans, he argues that Christ is the physical descendant of David (Rom 1:3). In Galatians 4:4, Paul asserts that Christ was born of a woman. This is in harmony with other biblical passages that teach the doctrine of the virgin birth of Jesus Christ. Furthermore in Philippians 2:8, Paul refers to Christ as "being found in human form."

The Deity of Jesus Christ

No other Pauline epistle explains the deity of Christ more than the epistle to the Colossians. In Colossians 1:15–17, Paul writes that the beloved Son of God "is the image of the invisible God." He is the one by whom and through whom and for whom all things were created. Later in Colossians 1:19, Paul asserts that in Christ "all the fullness of God was pleased to dwell." This idea is related to Colossians 2:9, where Paul says that in Christ "the whole fullness of deity dwells bodily." Another portion depicting the idea of Christ's deity is Philippians 2:6: Christ "was in the form of God." The idea here corresponds to Christ being in the very nature of God. This verse suggests the divinity and the eternity of Christ.

A number of times, Paul uses the term "the Son of God" to designate the deity of Christ. Christ is the eternal and only begotten Son of God. For this reason, he is equal with God the Father in respect to godhood. The gospel of God, Paul declares, is "concerning his Son, who was descended from David according to the flesh, and was declared to be the Son of God in power according to the Spirit of holiness by his resurrection from the dead, Jesus Christ our Lord" (Rom 1:3–4).

The Work of Jesus Christ

If death is the wages of sin, how could death be applicable to Christ since he "knew no sin" (2 Cor 5:21)? Certainly, he did not deserve to die. Yet he died. Isn't this a contradiction of him being God? Christ did die because of his obedience to the Father. In Philippians 2:8 Paul says of Christ, "And being found in human form, he humbled himself by becoming obedient to the point of death, even death on a cross." About these words, John Murray says that Paul "does not mean that he was obedient up to the point of death, but obedient to the extent of yielding up his life and dismissing his spirit in death. Death was the climactic requirement of his obedience."[20] Christ's obedience resides in being sent by the Father (Rom 8:3–4; Gal 4:4–5). He was sent to deal with sin and its consequences so that by his "obedience the many will be made righteous" (Rom 5:19).

The Holy Spirit

The Holy Spirit Is a Person

Paul states that the Holy Spirit can grieve (Eph 4:30); lead (Rom 8:14; Gal 5:18); bear witness (Rom 8:16); give help and intercede "for us with groanings too deep for words" (Rom 8:26); and cry to God on our behalf (Gal 4:6). Only a person can do such things. He is an individual person.

The Holy Spirit Is God

Some passages in the Pauline epistles make a connection between Father, Son, and Spirit together in the inseparable unity (1 Cor 12:4–6; 2 Cor 13:14; Eph 1:3–14; 2:18; 3:14–19; 4:4–6; 2 Thess 2:13–14). The Holy Spirit is God.

---

20. John Murray, *Collected Writings of John Murray: Volume One – The Claims of Truth* (Edinburgh: Banner of Truth, 1976), 37.

The Holy Spirit Regenerates

Paul refers to regeneration as "new creation" (2 Cor 5:17; Gal 6:15) and explains it in terms of union with Christ in his death and resurrection resulting in a changed life (Rom 6:3–11; Col 2:12–14). Everyone who believes the Lord Jesus Christ receives the Holy Spirit (Eph 1:13). At that moment he or she is regenerated by the Holy Spirit (Titus 3:4–7).

The Holy Spirit Seals

The term "seal" in reference to the Holy Spirit appears in many passages of Pauline epistles. Some examples include the following: "In him you also, when you heard the word of truth, the gospel of your salvation, and believed in him, were sealed with the promised Holy Spirit" (Eph 1:13); "And do not grieve the Holy Spirit of God, by whom you were sealed for the day of redemption" (Eph 4:30); and "It is God who establishes us with you in Christ, and has anointed us, and who has also put his seal on us and given us his Spirit in our hearts as a guarantee" (2 Cor 1:21–22).

These texts denote the reality that believers are owned by God. Since their spiritual baptism on the day of redemption, they now belong to God and are therefore secure and safe in him. Believers received a mark on the day of their spiritual resurrection – when they were regenerated by the Holy Spirit on the day he placed them into the body of Christ (1 Cor 12:13). This mark testifies to the indwelling of the Holy Spirit in the believer.

The Holy Spirit Indwells

Paul affirms that the indwelling of the Holy Spirit in believers is synonymous to their belonging to Christ (Rom 8:9). And the Holy Spirit inside us testifies to our spirit of the truth that as believers, we are children and heirs of God (Rom 8:15–17). As believers, we are the temple of the Holy Spirit and are called to glorify God in our body (1 Cor 6:19–20).

The Holy Spirit Sanctifies

Sanctification starts with our union with Christ. In Romans 6:10, Paul writes that "For the death [Christ] died he died to sin, once for all" (Rom 6:10). Believers also died to sin and live in newness of life (Rom 6:2, 5). Thus, believers are called to put to death the deeds of the body through the Holy Spirit so that they may live (Rom 8:13).

Humanity and Sin

In the book of Romans, Paul explains how both Jews and gentiles have failed to live up to the standards of God. Gentiles have the natural revelation, and the law is written on their hearts, and the Jews have the Mosaic law. But the two groups have failed in their attempts to be righteous. Thus, Paul argues that sin began when human beings knew God but "they did not honor him as God or give thanks to him, but they became futile in their thinking, and their foolish hearts were darkened" (Rom 1:21).

Later in this epistle Paul says, "For the mind that is set on the flesh is hostile to God, for it does not submit to God's law; indeed, it cannot" (Rom 8:7). Apart from Christ's redemptive work, our minds are darkened to spiritual things, our wills are alienated from God's will, and our consciences are insensitive to God's voice (Eph 4:18). We are perverse and ungodly (Rom 5:6), sinners are under God's wrath (Rom 1:18). In Ephesians 2, Paul stresses the idea that we "were dead in [our] trespasses and sins" (v. 1). This death came from Adam who ruined his life and his descendants' through his disobedience to God's instructions, "For as in Adam all die, so also in Christ shall all be made alive" (1 Cor 15:22).

Salvation

The word "salvation," in Greek *soteria*, carries the idea of deliverance from the perplexity of enemies. In his epistles, Paul does not only portray believers as delivered from sin (Rom 6:17–22), but also saved from the wrath of God: "Since, therefore, we have now been justified by his blood, much more shall we be saved by him from the wrath of God" (Rom 5:9). Salvation is explained here as deliverance from the wrath of God that is "revealed from heaven against all ungodliness and unrighteousness of men" (Rom 1:18).

This salvation is not received by an exchange between God and the recipient but is a gift of grace. In Ephesians 2:8 Paul says, "For by grace you have been saved through faith. And this is not your own doing; it is the gift of God." Thus it is the grace of God that brings salvation (Rom 5:15; Titus 2:11) that is to be received by faith in Jesus Christ (Rom 3:28).

The word "grace" is a translation of the Greek word *charis* which carries the sense of kindness bestowed to someone who does not deserve it. Thus, grace is the unmerited favor of God towards human beings in and through Jesus Christ (Rom 3:21–25). In Ephesians, Paul uses phrases like "the riches of his grace" (1:7; 2:7), "the riches of his glorious inheritance" (1:18), "the riches of his glory"

(3:16), and "the unsearchable riches of Christ" (3:8) to mean the same idea of God's undeserved favor. Paul uses other words to depict salvation as well.

Adoption

In Pauline writings, the word "adoption" denotes the nature of believers in Christ who by receiving the Holy Spirit become the children of God. In Ephesians 1:5, Paul says that God has "predestined us for adoption to himself as sons through Jesus Christ, according to the purpose of his will." But adoption also denotes the future consummation of believers' position as children of God. Paul says in Romans 8:23, "And not only the creation, but we ourselves, who have the firstfruits of the Spirit, groan inwardly as we wait eagerly for adoption as sons, the redemption of our bodies."

Redemption

Paul uses the term "redemption" to mean a deliverance procured by a payment of a ransom. This ransom is paid by Christ through his death for the forgiveness of our sins (Eph 1:7; Col 1:13–14). Paul also says that we are "justified by his grace as a gift, through the redemption that is in Christ Jesus" (Rom 3:24; see also Titus 3:4–7). In Paul's idea of redemption, we are not only forgiven through the shedding of the blood of Jesus Christ, but we are set free from the power of sin. Paul also stretches the term to the idea of total liberation from the power of sin that still affects believers (see Rom 8:23, where redemption is parallel to the glorification of Rom 8:30), the final consummation of our redemption.

Justification

We explained the term "justification" in the Pauline theology of God (see The Righteousness of God above). This term simply bears the sense of declaring someone to be just or righteous. Paul asserts that we as sinners are hostile to God (Rom 8:7), and we "all have sinned and fall short of the glory of God" (Rom 3:23). Because of our alienation from God, we are not able to do what is expected of us. Thus Paul explains that we are justified in Christ, "the end of the law for righteousness to everyone who believes" (Rom 10:4; see also Rom 3:21–26).

In different references, Paul lists the benefits of our justification. For example, believers are justified by the grace of God so that "we might become heirs according to the hope of eternal life" (Titus 3:7). People who have been alienated from God (Eph 2:12) now "have peace with God through our Lord Jesus Christ" (Rom 5:1). We have also by faith obtained access to God's undeserved favor and "rejoice in the hope of the glory of God" (5:2) as well as in trials and tribulations (5:3).

The Last Things

Most of Paul's teaching on eschatology is concerned about the future glorification of the believer (Rom 8:17) rather than the events or circumstances preceding the second coming of Christ. The themes of hope and judgment are also predominant in Paul's writings. For example in Titus 2:11–13, Paul explains, "For the grace of God has appeared, bringing salvation for all people, training us to renounce ungodliness and worldly passions, and to live self-controlled, upright, and godly lives in the present age, waiting for our blessed hope, the appearing of the glory of our great God and savior Jesus Christ." Alister McGrath says, "Paul looks forward to the future coming of Jesus Christ in judgment at the end of time, confirming the new life of believers and their triumph over sin and death. . . . For Paul, there is an intimate connection between the final coming of Christ and the execution of final judgment."[21]

Elsewhere, Paul explains how the hope of eternal life is laid up in heaven for both the living and the dead in Christ (1 Thess 4:16–17), the great Judge. Paul says that the dead in Christ will rise first, and then those who are alive at Christ's coming will be caught up with them. Paul continues by saying that the moment of Christ's final coming is unknown and hidden from all (1 Thess 5:1–3). At his final coming, the Lord Jesus Christ "will transform our lowly body to be like his glorious body" (Phil 3:21). And then we "will appear with him in glory" (Col 3:4).

In his second letter to the Thessalonians, Paul describes what will happen to the people who do not know God. The apostle asserts, "They will suffer the punishment of eternal destruction, away from the presence of the Lord and from the glory of his might" (2 Thess 1:9).

---

21. McGrath, *Christian Theology*, 428.

2

Metaphoric Figures of the Church

Early in my seminary years, a teacher of a homiletics class would always remind us of these words on preaching: "Don't just tell them; you have to show them as well." For the teacher, a preacher must translate the gospel in words and in actions in ways that those listening will see and will appreciate it; he must allow them to drink from his labor. In the preface of my King James Version Bible of 1611, the translators also emphasize the importance of translation with these words.

> Translation it is that openeth the window, to let in the light; that breaketh the shell, that we may eat the kernel; that putteth aside the curtain, that we may look into the most Holy place; that removeth the cover of the well, that we may come by the water, even as Jacob rolled away the stone from the mouth of the well, by which means the flocks of Laban were watered [Gen. 29:10]. Indeed without translation into the vulgar tongue, the unlearned are but like children at Jacob's well (which is deep) [John 4:11] without a bucket or something to draw with; or as that person mentioned by Isaiah, to whom when a sealed book was delivered, with this motion, "Read this, I pray thee," he was fain to make this answer, "I cannot, for it is sealed." [Isa. 29:11]

According to these translators, translation is about unpacking the meaning of words in ways that connect up with people in your culture. It is about removing the curtain of ignorance in order to shade the light of knowledge. Translation is all about letting people drink from the well they are not able to access by themselves. However, translating is more than saying the best English words for different Greek or Hebrew words. It is also about explaining complex words in ways that make sense to the culture around you.

One of the ways of communicating meaning is the use of metaphors. Metaphors are a means by which you express an understanding of complex concepts. Since the Bible was written by human authors from different cultures, they found it necessary to use metaphors to communicate to their audiences. The Old Testament, especially its poetic literature, is filled with metaphoric expressions that explain the nature of God. Furthermore, Paul uses metaphors to explain hard concepts, like the mystery of the church, to help his audience grasp its meaning. Hence, his use of metaphors helps us understand the reality of our union with Christ.

In this chapter, we will focus on the different metaphors Paul uses to express the church of God. Whereas his audience, mainly believing Jews and gentiles, wrestled with the complexities of the mystery of the church, Paul clarified its meaning through the use of metaphors. Here we will go through different passages of the Bible describing the metaphoric images Paul ascribes to the mystery of the church. As we will see, each metaphor carries an idea that describes the complexity of the relationship between Christ and the church. Alister McGrath explains that "when finite minds encounter infinite reality, they struggle to express what they encounter. Using analogies is one way of coping with this, allowing our fallen and finite minds to grasp enough of the reality of God to keep us going in our faith."[1]

Definition of the Church

In his first letter, Paul addresses the Corinthian congregation with these words: "To the church of God that is in Corinth, to those sanctified in Christ Jesus, called to be saints together with those who in every place call upon the name of our Lord Jesus Christ, both their Lord and ours" (1 Cor 1:2). In this verse, Paul equates the church of God to the people who are *sanctified in Christ Jesus* or those who are *called to be saints*.

Paul wrote this letter to a group of people who had been called by God to be saints. This group of people was to be found *in* Corinth. They are not called saints *of* Corinth but saints *in* Corinth. The preposition "in" carries the idea of universality. Paul uses the same preposition in other letters to express the oneness of the church in different places. For instance in the book of Romans, Paul writes, "To all those in Rome who are loved by God and called to be saints" (Rom 1:7). Again he does not say "to those *of* Rome" as if they are different from the rest of the world. Also in the book of Ephesians, Paul writes, "To the saints

---

1. Alister McGrath, *The Living God: Christian Belief for Everyone* (London: SPCK, 2013), 22.

who are *in* Ephesus, and are faithful in Christ Jesus" (Eph 1:1). Even though in the books of Philippians and Colossians the preposition changes to "*at*" (Phil 1:1; Col 1:2), it still expresses the same idea of the universality of the people who are called by God. The prepositions "in" and "at" are interchangeably used by Paul to show that the church is one despite their dispersion (1 Pet 1:1) in different places. Millard Erickson writes,

> Paul uses the word *ekklesia* more than does any other New Testament writer. Since the majority of his writings were letters addressed to specific local gatherings of believers, it is not surprising that the term usually refers to a group of believers in a specific city . . . the opening portion of John's Apocalypse (Rev 1–3) was addressed to seven specific churches. In Acts, also, *ekklesia* refers primarily to all Christians who live and meet in a particular city, such as Jerusalem (Acts 5:11; 8:1; 11:22; 12:1, 5) or Antioch (13:1).[2]

The apostle Paul wrote all his epistles to the same people, namely the called or the saints found in different places. "Called" (Greek: *kletos*) refers to the invitation that God extends to people so that, through their positive response, they may be united to Christ. These people are called to be saints; they are called by God, through the redemptive work of Christ, to belong to him. In this sense, they are set apart to belong exclusively to God. Just as the people of Israel were a nation set apart for God to live a life favorable to him and distinct from other nations, believers are referred to as people whom God has chosen through the redemptive work of Christ that through the power of the Holy Spirit they may belong to God and live a holy and acceptable life before him.

Thus we may define the church as an assembly of people who have been called by God to belong to him and to worship him out of a passion for holiness and Christ likeness. Along these lines, Paul Enns writes that "the English word church also translates the Greek *ekklesia*, which is derived from *ek*, meaning 'out of,' and *kaleo*, which means 'to call'; hence, the church is 'a called-out group.'"[3]

---

2. Millard J. Erickson, *Christian Theology* (Grand Rapids: Baker Academic, 2013), 956.

3. Paul Enns, *The Moody Handbook of Theology*, rev. ed. (Chicago: Moody, 2008), 358.

The Visible Church and the Invisible Church

Since the time of the church fathers, theologians have tried to establish the relationship between the visible church and the invisible church. On the one hand, theologians have argued that only God knows the people who belong to him. Thus this group which is known only by God is the invisible church. On the other hand, the people who gather together in a certain locality are the visible church since it is so hard to tell who are the elect of God and who are not. Therefore, the invisible church is inclusive in the visible church.

But this distinction does not clearly appear in the Bible. Since we have defined the church as the "assembly of the people who have been called by God to belong to him," I am hesitant in this book to refer to the church in terms of visibility and invisibility. Furthermore, it is my conviction that there are no strong biblical evidences for the notion of the church as an invisible group of people distinct from the church as visible. John Murray gives, in my opinion, a strong argument on this point,

> Strictly speaking, it is not proper to speak of the "invisible church." According to Scripture we should speak of "the church" and conceive it as that visible entity that exists and functions in accord with the institution of Christ as its Head, the church that is the body of Christ indwelt and directed by the Holy Spirit, consisting of those sanctified in Christ Jesus and called to be saints, manifested in the congregations of the faithful, and finally the church glorious, holy and without blemish.[4]

The Church as God's Building

> For we are God's fellow workers. You are God's field, God's building. According to the grace of God given to me, like a skilled *master builder* I laid a *foundation*, and someone else is *building* upon it. Let each one take care how he builds upon it. For no one can lay a *foundation* other than that which is laid, which is Jesus Christ. Now if anyone builds on the *foundation* with gold, silver, precious stones, wood, hay, straw – each one's work will become manifest, for the Day will disclose it, because it will be revealed by fire, and the fire will test what sort of work each one has done.

---

4. John Murray, *Collected Writings of John Murray: Volume One – The Claims of Truth* (Edinburgh: Banner of Truth, 1976), 236.

> If the work that anyone has built on the *foundation* survives, he will receive a reward. If anyone's work is burned up, he will suffer loss, though he himself will be saved, but only as through fire. (1 Cor 3:9–15)

In the book of 1 Corinthians, the apostle Paul found it necessary to address many practical questions that were dividing the church and to correct problems as well as false teaching concerning Jesus Christ. In the book of Acts, we see the man who "was ravaging the church" (Acts 8:3). But in 1 Corinthians we find the same man, namely Paul, who God is divinely using to build the church on Jesus Christ as the foundation. However, coming to the third chapter of the book, we see that one of the problems that had risen in the church of Corinth was division. The people within the church started to form cliques according to personalities. Some were claiming to belong to Paul, others to Apollos, some to Cephas, and still others to Jesus Christ. In realizing this division, Paul was compelled to write to them and set the issue by reminding them that they are the building upon which Christ Jesus is the foundation. Walter Kaiser suggests that

> The splits represented by these various parties do not seem to represent doctrinal divisions, for in that case Paul would have addressed those doctrinal aberrations. But there is no word about such potential heresy. Instead, it seems to be more a matter of boasting about prestigious personalities and rallying to them rather than maintaining the unity of the body in the midst of their diversity.[5]

In 1 Corinthians 3:5–9, Paul reminds the Corinthians that it is wrong to make cliques in the church since Paul, Apollos, and Cephas are *fellow workers* in building up *God's building*, the church. Thus Paul put himself on the same level with other builders by considering them as companions in the work. He recognized the fact that all who labor together in furthering the cause of Christ are all one, as is also the case for Epaphroditus whom Paul calls a "fellow worker" (Phil 2:25). Paul considered all people who share the ministry of building the Christian community as co-workers. He did not consider certain functions or ministries within the church as superior to others.

By the providence of God, Paul was a missionary who planted many churches along the Mediterranean, including the church of Corinth. Thus

---

5. Walter C. Kaiser, Jr., *The Promise-Plan of God: A Biblical Theology of the Old and New Testaments* (Grand Rapids: Zondervan, 2008), 271.

Paul claimed to have laid down the foundation; but not in the same sense as Jesus Christ (1 Cor 3:11). Paul laid the foundation in the sense that he, as a preacher, was the first to bring the gospel to the Corinthians and plant a church there. He says later in the book, "I would remind you, brothers, of the gospel I preached to you, which you received, in which you stand, and by which you are being saved, if you hold fast to the word I preached to you – unless you believed in vain" (1 Cor 15:1–2).

Someone else built upon the foundation. In other words, through his missionary work, Paul established this body of Christians in Corinth by proclaiming to them the first principles of the Christian life and doctrine. And someone else, a fellow worker in the kingdom of God, built upon this foundation by edifying the believers so that they grew in Christian wisdom, piety, holiness, etc.

To build is to erect a building from the foundation up. In this passage, Paul is using the image of a building to mean the church. But he affirms that this building is built upon the foundation which is the Lord Jesus Christ because "no one can lay a foundation other than that which is laid, which is Jesus Christ" (1 Cor 3:11). Thus building up the church depends on Jesus Christ, the foundation of its existence. As far as the church is concerned, no other foundation is logically possible except the Lord Jesus Christ who declared that he will build his church, "and the gates of hell shall not prevail against it" (Matt 16:18).

Christ Jesus lays himself in the soul of believers as the foundation of their faith. The author of Hebrews says that Jesus Christ is "the founder and perfecter of our faith, who for the joy that was set before him endured the cross, despising the shame, and is seated at the right hand of the throne of God" (Heb 12:2). It is upon Christ that our building of the Christian community must be erected. In 2 Corinthians 1:24, Paul writes "Not that we lord it over your faith, but we work with you for your joy, for you stand firm in your faith."

The ultimate goal of Paul and his fellow workers was to build up the church on the one foundation, Jesus Christ. But Paul ends this part with a warning against those who build on another foundation other than Jesus. God alone will judge how each Christian contributes to the work of building the church. But woe to the person who divides the church, for "If anyone's work is burned up, he will suffer loss, though he himself will be saved, but only as through fire" (1 Cor 3:15). Paul compares this person's work to *wood*, *hay*, and *straw* that do not resist fire (3:12). But those who have built on Jesus Christ as their foundation will receive a divine recompense. Paul compares this person's work to *gold*, *silver*, and *precious stones* which become purer in the testing of fire (3:12–13).

The Church as God's Temple

> Do you not know that you are God's temple and that God's Spirit dwells in you? If anyone destroys God's temple, God will destroy him. For God's temple is holy, and you are that temple. (1 Cor 3:16–17)

In 1 Corinthians 3, Paul now moves away from the metaphor of the building to describe the community of Christians as the temple. The rhetorical question "*Do you not know?*" which we find in the beginning of verse 16 introduces a new metaphor. With this question, Paul probably wanted to remind the Corinthian believers of what they had been told before rather than trying to tell them a new reality. And Paul shows that the church is not just any building but in fact God's temple in which the Holy Spirit dwells.

We should keep in mind here that Paul is still addressing the Corinthians. Thus, the pronoun in the 3:16 must be plural "Do *you* [plural] not know that *you* [plural] are God's temple and that God's Spirit dwells in *you* [plural]?" This verse should not be interpreted in the same way as the idea of an individual as the temple of the Spirit in 1 Corinthians 6:19. In verse 3:16, the image must be taken to mean that the Spirit dwells in the midst of the Christian community.

The church is the community of believers indwelt by the Spirit. And when they gather in his name, God should be worshiped in such a way that his presence and power are manifested through their unity and harmony. Paul stresses this idea in Ephesians 2:21–22, "in whom the whole structure, being joined together, grows into a holy temple in the Lord. In him you also are being built together into a dwelling place for God by the Spirit."

In 1 Corinthians 3:17, Paul then introduces a syllogism to show what will happen to those who seek to destroy the unity of the church. We can paraphrase the verse in this way:

> God's temple is holy.
> *Yet* you are the temple.
> *Thus, you are holy.*

God's elect people have been made holy in Christ, and the Holy Spirit dwells in them. Therefore, no one should corrupt or defile the temple lest God destroy them. The church, this harmonious community of Christians, has been set apart to belong to God. The destroyers of the temple are those who want to shatter the Spirit out of the community. They probably want to oppose the fruit of the Spirit through their works of the flesh, "sexual immorality, impurity, sensuality . . . strife, jealousy, fits of anger, rivalries, dissensions" etc. (Gal 5:19–21). They destroy by means of their immoral and depraved influences. Anthony Thiselton argues that, "Paul warns the addressees that seriously to undo the work of authentic building thereby brings destruction upon the person in question, and thereby also invites the corroborative verdict of the judgment of God. That person's plight is dreadful indeed."[6]

The Church as the Bride of Christ[7]

> Husbands, love your wives, as Christ loved the church and gave himself up for her, that he might sanctify her, having cleansed her by the washing of water with the word, so that he might present the church to himself in splendor, without spot or wrinkle or any such thing, that she might be holy and without blemish. (Eph 5:25–27)

The apostle Paul has a very clear and stunning structure in his epistles. For instance, the book of Ephesians is divided into two parts. The first three chapters talk about what God has done for the church, and the last three chapters talk about what we are called to do in light of what God has done. In other words, the first part is doctrinal, and the second is more practical. We will explore this structure more in the next chapter.

Throughout the book of Ephesians, love is one of the predominant themes, with an emphasis right at the beginning on God's great love for us stretching back all the way to eternity past. In eternity past, God set his affection on a people. God's love for his people stretches back even before the world begin. But the book of Ephesians also emphasizes how we then as God's people are to love each other.

For example, in Christ we are blessed "with every spiritual blessing" (Eph 1:3). In Christ we are "holy and blameless before him" (1:4). In Christ "we have redemption through his blood, the forgiveness of our trespasses" (1:7). In Christ we are "sealed with the promised Holy Spirit" (1:13). In Christ we "are alive together with Christ" (2:5). In Christ we were created for good

---

6. Anthony C. Thiselton, *The First Epistle to the Corinthians: The New International Greek Testament Commentary* (Grand Rapids: Eerdmans, 2000), 318.

7. On the church as the body of Christ, see Constantine R. Campbell, *Paul and Union with Christ: An Exegetical and Theological Study* (Grand Rapids: Zondervan, 2012), 63–64, 268–289.

works (2:10). In Christ we "are fellow citizens with the saints and members of the household of God" (2:19). In Christ "we have boldness and access with confidence through our faith in him" (3:12). All these blessings have become ours in Christ because of God's love for us.

One of the great marks of believers in Christ is God's love flowing in and through them. Every believer is called to let this love flow in themselves and to others so that the church grows. In other words, love is a grace that all Christians are to exercise with each other, and it is an identifying feature in the fellowship of God's people. Thus because of God's love, believers are expected to have mutual cooperation between themselves; they are to be indivisible and uncorrupted.

Paul expands this idea of Christ's love into the marriage setting. He asserts that Christ's sacrificial love should be the model by which husbands are to love their wives. When we talk about marriage, we should keep in mind who God is and what he has done in Christ because it is the foundation of the husband's motivation to love his wife. Only as both a husband and wife understand what God has done can they properly fulfill their different roles in marriage.

Christ sacrificed himself for us, we who were dead in sins (Eph 2:1); he died for us so that we may be resurrected with him. We are no longer in the grave of our trespasses; neither do we wander in the cemetery of our sins. We are seated with God "in the heavenly places in Christ Jesus" (Eph 2:6). Christ dwells in our hearts in order to display his sacrificial love in and through us. Thus when we understand the depth of the love of Christ, we will be filled with an attitude of obedience and reverence to him. Christ did not come to obligate us to obey him; but since he has revealed to us the magnitude of his grace, we are being compelled to obey him not out of force but out of gratitude. In the same way, Paul argues, this should be the way husbands love their wives. In this way, marriage should be a picture of our union with Christ.

I should emphasize here that a distorted and damaged understanding of Christ's relationship with his church might distort the way we view marriage. If we don't understand Christ's union with his church, we may give in to unbiblical, cultural, or traditional understandings of marriage. If we have a poor view of Christ and his redemptive work, we may abuse our roles in marriage.

The church is a group of people who truly are in Christ. These people have been redeemed by Christ, and they belong to him. Paul takes us further when he says, "the husband is the head of the wife even as Christ is the head of the church" (Eph 5:23). Christ, the image of the invisible God, the exact representation of his being and nature, came down to die for the redemption and sanctification of his bride, the church. If you've been saved by Christ, you are part of the church, the Christian community.

Paul ends Ephesians 5 with a quote from the book of Genesis, "Therefore a man shall leave his father and mother and hold fast to his wife, and the two shall become one flesh" (Eph 5:31; Gen 2:24). When we exchange vows on our wedding day, "For better and for worse, in sickness and in health, in richness and in poverty, till death do us apart," we are making a commitment to be one flesh, an illustration of Christ's commitment to us. Christ and his bride, the church, have inseparably become one.

The church has been united with Christ through his death, and for this reason he will never leave her nor forsake her, because "he gave himself up for her, that he might sanctify her, having cleansed her by the washing of water with the word, so that he might present the church to himself in splendor, without spot or wrinkle or any such thing, that she might be holy and without blemish" (Eph 5:25–27). Constantine Campbell writes, "the metaphorical joining of husband and wife and their becoming one flesh indicate a profound union between Christ and the church. The metaphor is personal and implies a bond of intimacy that goes well beyond the other metaphors that Paul uses in portraying union with Christ."[8]

The union between Christ and his bride, the church, finds its climactic expression in the new Jerusalem – "prepared as a bride adorned for her husband" (Rev 21:2) – which is characterized not by Jews only but by a glorified people from different tongues and nations who have been united to Christ. The church, the bride of Christ and city of God, will be the new covenant temple since "its temple is the Lord God the Almighty and the Lamb" (Rev 21:22).

In conclusion, the theme of the church is prevalent in almost every Pauline epistle, with a particular emphasis on its theology. In the book of Ephesians, Paul shows how in eternity past God set his affection on a people to belong to him, back even before the world began (Eph 1:4–6). In other chapters of the same book, Paul stretches the idea that the church is composed of both Jews and gentiles who are fellow heirs of the promise and members of the same body of Christ (2:19; 3:6).

---

8. Campbell, *Paul and Union with Christ*, 308.

The Church as the Body of Christ

Campbell affirms that "the body of Christ is one of Paul's most important metaphors for describing the nature of the church."[9] Paul drew this metaphor from the anatomy of the human body. He pictured the church as a set of structures that make up the human body and how those structures relate with each other. It is crucial to emphasize that Paul was not referring to the physical body of Christ which was born of the virgin Mary, crucified, buried, and resurrected. The body of Christ depicts the church of God – a unity of believers relating with one another and dependent on Christ as the head of the body. There are two things we can learn from the human body that help us better understand the nature of the church.

Dependence on the Head

From the study of anatomy, we know that the control of the body's billion cells is accomplished mainly by the head via the nervous system. In the same way, the body of Christ can only function when Christ, the head, is present. Otherwise, we cannot call it a body. Paul wrote in Colossians, "And he is the head of the body, the church. He is the beginning, the firstborn from the dead, that in everything he might be preeminent" (Col 1:18). There is no time when we can think of the church without its head, Christ Jesus. If we think of a church without Christ, we are guilty of idolatry, and it is not the church.

Christ is the head of the church as the head is to the human body. This implies that Christ assumes certain functions to keep the church alive. In other words, the church completely depends on Christ for life.

1. As the head of the body, Christ is the Savior of the body (Eph 5:23). This is why Christ gave his life for the redemption of his own body, the church.

2. The body, the church of God, grows by "holding fast to the Head" (Col 2:19). As the head of the church, Christ is the source of all knowledge and wisdom. It is by constantly clinging to him that the church grows.

---

9. Campbell, 268.

Interrelatedness of the Members

Paul wrote to the church in Corinth, "For just as the body is one and has many members, and all the members of the body, though many, are one body, so it is with Christ. . . . Now you are the body of Christ and individually members of it" (1 Cor 12:12, 27). We are not going to bring into the conversation every notion of anatomy and physiology, but these two sciences reveal that the human body has different structures of organization such as for atoms, cells, tissues, and organs and systems that make up the complete organism. Though believers are distinct from one another, they constitute the different parts of the body as an organism. Campbell puts it this way,

> The union that believers have with Christ has a totalizing effect on the one hand, and a distinguishing effect on the other. Believers are the body of Christ; they are all made into one, forming a single corporate identity. But believers are also individual parts of the body; their unity together does not quash their distinct and diverse otherness.[10]

Paul wrote to the church at Rome, "For as in one body we have many members, and the members do not all have the same function, so we, though many, are one body in Christ, and individually members one of another" (Rom 12:4–5). As none of the body systems are capable of functioning alone, so believers cannot function individually in their closet. They are to be interdependent and must work together as one unit so that normal conditions within the church may prevail.

Therefore all members of the church are to exercise their gifts for the edification of the church,

> Having gifts that differ according to the grace given to us, let us use them; if prophecy, in proportion to our faith; if service, in our serving; the one who teaches, in his teaching; the one who exhorts, in his exhortation; the one who contributes, in generosity; the one who leads, with zeal; the one who does acts of mercy, with cheerfulness. (Rom 12:6–8)

God has given gifts "to each one individually as he wills" (1 Cor 12:11) "for building up the body of Christ" (Eph 4:12). Erickson writes,

> The body is to be characterized by genuine fellowship. This does not mean social interrelatedness, but an intimate feeling for and

---

10. Campbell, *Paul and Union with Christ*, 274.

understanding of one another. . . . One aspect of the body of Christ that has been inadequately emphasized is that fellowship extends across time. . . . The body is to be a unified body. . . . All ethnic and social barriers have been removed.[11]

As Christ cares for those united to him as members of his body, so the members are to care for one another. The church is also called to unity in service. The members are to pray for one another "making supplication for all the saints" (Eph 6:18). They are to hold each other in prayer because of the battle Satan is raging against them. That's how they show the unity of the body.

The Church as a Flock

> Pay careful attention to yourselves and to all the flock, in which the Holy Spirit has made you overseers, to care for the church of God, which he obtained with his own blood. (Acts 20:28)

Luke records Paul's third missionary journey including Paul's three-year ministry in Ephesus before he was arrested in Jerusalem. Paul found it necessary to encourage the elders of the church in Ephesus to take seriously the responsibility God had entrusted to them, to take care of the flock. In the New Testament, the Greek word translated "flock" is *poimnion* which denotes a body of Christians presided over by elders.

In this passage, Paul makes a comparison between a flock and the church of God. Thus, he urges the shepherds, the elders, *to pay careful attention to themselves*. The elders are to be watchful of the dangers around them. As shepherds, they are also to be very sensitive to the dangers that come against the flock under their care. They are to be alert to any spiritual danger that may harm the church of God.

In order to pay careful attention, the elders are to exercise self-control. Paul expresses this idea in 1 Timothy 3:2–3, "Therefore an overseer must be above reproach, the husband of one wife, sober-minded, self-controlled, respectable, hospitable, able to teach, not a drunkard, not violent but gentle, not quarrelsome, not a lover of money." Contrary to a drunken soldier who cannot stay on watch and lets the enemy slip in, the elders in Ephesus are to be watchful because of the devil's snares and schemes. They are to control their passions; they are not to be involved in fanciful actions that will destroy the welfare of the people of God.

---

11. Erickson, *Christian Theology*, 961.

Paul needed to remind these elders that Satan, the roaring lion, is hostile to the flock and that they should be watchful for destructive attacks against the church of God. Similarly in warning elders, the apostle Peter wrote, "I exhort the elders among you . . . shepherd the flock of God that is among you, exercising oversight, not under compulsion, but willingly, as God would have you; not for shameful gain, but eagerly; not domineering over those in your charge, but being examples to the flock" (1 Pet 5:1–3).

Elders are to take seriously their responsibility to tend the flock in both conduct and in the word of God for two major reasons. First, overseers have been entrusted by the Holy Spirit to lead the people of God. Paul considered elders to be commissioned by God himself. This ministry is not conferred on them by human beings but by the Holy Spirit. Second, there is an urgency for elders to tend the flock because it is the church of God which he purchased for himself through the blood of his beloved Son.

To Paul and Peter, the image of the flock emphasizes the members of the church. This is in connection with what Jesus said in John 10:14–16, "I am the good shepherd. I know my own and my own know me, just as the Father knows me and I know the Father; and I lay down my life for the sheep. And I have other sheep that are not of this fold. I must bring them also, and they will listen to my voice. So there will be one flock, one shepherd." The last words in this passage carry the truth about the church. The flock is not only composed of the Jewish sheep. The good shepherd has other sheep from other nations that belong to the flock, the church of God. Thus Jesus Christ communicates a profound truth: the coming of the Jews and the gentiles to be one flock under one shepherd, "the chief Shepherd" (1 Pet 5:4). This is what Paul preached while going from one end of the Mediterranean to the other. We shall develop this truth in the next chapter. On this topic, C. K. Barrett says in his commentary on John 10:16,

> For John, the unity of the one flock is not a given unity naturally existing, but a unity created in and by Jesus . . . as it indicates by the first part of this verse, his primary thought is on the unity of Jew and Gentile in the church. . . . He also emphasizes again, as frequently, the unity of believers with Christ and of Christ with the Father.[12]

---

12. C. K. Barrett, *The Gospel According to John: An Introduction with Commentary and Notes on the Greek Text* (London: SPCK, 1955), 313.

3

The Mystery of the Church
Ephesians 3:1–12

Introduction to the Book of Ephesians

Given the different figures of the church, it is now appropriate to study one of the great themes in Paul's writings – *the mystery of the church*. Constantine Campbell says that "Paul was a theologian and, while not 'systematic' in modern terms, he presented his thinking through the interaction of themes that are broader than the use of so-called formulas. Consequently, a proper approach to Paul must be theological as well as exegetical."[1] It is my conviction that to understand Paul's thinking on this mystery, a careful study of his epistles is appropriate. Therefore, I have chosen the epistle to the Ephesians as a study book to better understand the mystery of the church.

Any thoughtful study of Pauline epistles will reveal a formidable structure. Most of his epistles can be divided into two parts: the theology and the practice. In the first part, Paul always stresses the doctrine that forms the foundation on which the practice is built. The first part tells believers of what has been done for them. In other words, it speaks of what God has done through Christ Jesus. The second part focuses on what believers must do in light of what has been done for them. This part is full of imperatives such as commands, instructions, or begging which are motivated by the indicatives like facts which are contained in the first part.

As we delve into a careful study of the book of Ephesians, we should keep this structure in mind. In our English Bible, the book of Ephesians can be divided in two parts: chapters 1–3 deal with doctrine. This section starts with

---

1. Constantine R. Campbell, *Paul and Union with Christ: An Exegetical and Theological Study* (Grand Rapids: Zondervan, 2012), 23.

a doxology, "Blessed be the God and Father of our Lord Jesus Christ, who has blessed us in Christ with every spiritual blessing in the heavenly places" (Eph 1:3) and ends with another, "Now to him who is able to do far more abundantly than all that we ask or think, according to the power at work within us, to him be glory in the church and in Christ Jesus throughout all generations, forever and ever. Amen" (3:20–21). This first section depicts the identity or the new position of believers in Christ Jesus. Through the redemptive work of Christ, believers have been made one with Christ.

The practical section, chapters 4–6, are a wake-up call for believers "to walk in a manner worthy of the calling to which you have been called" (Eph 4:1). This is a call to a holy life because of who God is and what he has done in Christ; he has predestined believers for adoption (1:5); believers have obtained redemption and forgiveness of trespasses through the blood of Jesus Christ (1:7); God has predestined them "according to the purpose of him who works all things according to the counsel of his will" (1:11), etc. Based on their position in Christ, believers find the motivation to do what they have been called to do. Their actions are not a result of self-righteousness but a response to who God is and what he has done in Christ. The position of believers in Christ is complete; they are saints who through the work of the Holy Spirit are becoming what they already are in Christ.

A Special Problem

There is more in the book of Ephesians. If the book of Acts deals with the history of the church, the book of Ephesians deals with its theology – the origin, the nature, the identity, and the future of the church are all found in this epistle. It tells how in eternity past, God set his affection on certain people to be his church, "he has chosen us in him before the foundation of the world, that we should be holy and blameless before him" (Eph 1:4).

Many theologians have wrestled with the question of the origin of the church. There is still the debate on the continuity and discontinuity of the church in the scholastic world. When did the church start? Did the church start as Israel in the Old Testament and continued in the New Testament as the new Israel? Did the church start with Abraham being called out to be a blessing to many nations? Or did the church start on the day of Pentecost when the Holy Spirit was poured out?

Any attempt to study the church considering the Old Testament will always raise the debate of continuity and discontinuity. According to Alister McGrath, "the church has always stressed its historical and theological continuity with the people of Israel."[2] Although I do not intend to delve into this debate, it is obvious to see that the Bible supports both views – the continuity and discontinuity of the church. The question is in what senses we see continuity and in what senses we see discontinuity.

The Mystery of the Church

The idea of religious associations was common among the Jews before and during the ministry of Jesus Christ. The union of the Jews and gentiles as equal in the church was to the Jews an impossible condition. Despite the Old Testament accounts concerning the salvation of gentiles (see below), Jews could not have believed that one day, all would be equal in Christ. Thus Paul, while still in a Roman prison because of the truth he preached (Eph 3:1; 4:1; 6:20), found it necessary to address the Ephesians about the unity of the church with a special focus on the mystery of Christ.

Paul identified himself, along with other "holy apostles and prophets" (Eph 3:5), as the revealer of the mystery. By his grace and great will, God revealed to him the truth concerning divine things that were unknown before. In other words, through the work of the Holy Spirit, God revealed to Paul his divine plan for the salvation of the gentiles. Thus Paul considered himself as a steward of this revelation, namely the mystery of the church. He considered this mystery as a dispensation by which the grace of God was given to him to carry out the secret purpose of God. By grace, God entrusted Paul with the duty of proclaiming the mystery of the church (Col 1:24–26).

In this revelation, Paul discovered that both Jews and gentiles are very much alike in Christ. He found out that in God's plan for salvation, both Jews and gentiles "are fellow heirs, members of the same body" (Eph 3:6). And Paul calls this a mystery because it "was not made known to the sons of men in other generations as it has now been revealed to his holy apostles and prophets by the Spirit" (3:5). As this verse implies, Paul was not the unique New Testament apostle to receive this revelation.

Paul describes gentiles as "alienated from the commonwealth of Israel and strangers to the covenants of promises, having no hope and without God in the world" (Eph 2:12). But all that has changed. They have come to know God and be known by God; they have been justified by God and are now "partakers of the promise in Christ Jesus through the gospel" (3:6). With this revelation,

---

2. Alister McGrath, *Christian Theology: An Introduction*, 6th ed. (Chichester: John Wiley, 2017), 354.

Paul deeply moves us out from the Judaic mindset to a more unified church thinking, the body of Christ.

Old Testament Accounts about the Gentiles

Why does Paul call the equal union of Jews and gentiles a mystery? Does this mean that the Old Testament saints knew nothing about the salvation of the gentiles? In one sense, the coming of gentiles to faith in God was predicted in the Old Testament. Thus, the mystery of the church was not *completely* new to the Old Testaments saints. Let us examine some Old Testament passages and see what they teach about the union of the gentiles with Jesus.

"I will bless those who bless you, and him who dishonors you I will curse, and in you all the families of the earth shall be blessed" (Gen 12:3). Of all the families of the earth, God elected Abraham to be a father of a nation that would serve God as priests to other nations of the world. In Exodus 19:6, God reminds the Israelites, "you shall be to me a kingdom of priests and a holy nation." A priest is a mediator representing the people to God. In that sense, the nation of Israel was to represent God before the nations that they might know God and be saved. The blessing of nations through Abraham indicates that the mystery was not entirely new.

Through Abraham, God made a nation from whom came the Messiah who would carry out the blessing of the nations. Paul stresses the idea that through Jesus Christ, the blessing of Abraham has come to the gentiles: "Christ redeemed us from the curse of the law by becoming a curse for us – for it is written, 'Cursed is everyone who is hanged on a tree' – so that in Christ Jesus the blessing of Abraham might come to the Gentiles, so that we might receive the promised Spirit through faith" (Gal 3:13–14). The redemptive work of Christ has brought the blessing of salvation to the gentiles as God promised to Abraham. God has brought the gentiles near through the work of Christ.

> Enlarge the place of your tent,
>   and let the curtains of your habitations be stretched out;
> do not hold back; lengthen your cords
>   and strengthen your stakes.
> For you will spread abroad to the right and the left,
>   and your offspring will possess the nations
>   and will people the desolate cities. (Isa 54:2–3)

This passage talks of when Israel will be enlarged to have accommodation also for the nations. The nations are outside the tent. They are without a shelter to dwell under. Jerome says, "Anyone who is in a tent does not have a secure and everlasting dwelling but is always changing places and hurrying on to the next."[3] The prophet is anticipating when the gentiles will be accommodated in this eternal home.

The prophet Isaiah gives us a picture of the Jews and gentiles dwelling together in the same tent. In this sense, by enlarging their tent to the ends of the earth, they will be able to accommodate the nations. The Israelites are to proclaim the glory of the Lord to the nations since they are a kingdom of priests. And by doing this, other nations will be enabled to be under the care of the God of Israel. These nations will benefit from the privileges provided to those who dwell in the tent.

> And nations shall come to your light
>   and kings to the brightness of your rising. (Isa 60:3)

In the Bible, light depicts knowledge of the Lord who gives understanding of himself and of the human self. The psalmist wrote, "The LORD is my light and my salvation" (Ps 27:1). Light is used to express the illumination that happens when people come to the knowledge of God and his salvation. Look for example at Acts 26:17–18: "I am sending you to open their eyes, so that they may turn from darkness to light and from the power of Satan to God, that they may receive forgiveness of sins and a place among those who are sanctified by faith in me."

Thus the prophet Isaiah was anticipating the coming of the Messiah who would enlighten the nations living in spiritual darkness. This light is life itself – true spiritual life, which gives gentiles peace, joy, and fellowship with God and one another for all eternity. By believing in the Messiah, the nations will step out of the darkness. They will move from ignorance to the knowledge of God. The prophet was anticipating the day the Messiah would bring a revelation about God to the nations. But the Messiah would be more than a revealer. He would himself be that revelation. In John 12:46, Jesus says, "I have come into the world as light, so that whoever believes in me may not remain in darkness."

The Bible teaches us that both Jews and gentiles are by nature rebellious toward God (Eph 2:1–3) and that everyone is guilty of sin and incapable of changing their sinful condition. Paul describes sinners as dead in their trespasses and sins (Eph 2:1). God's love for us has provided a Savior who died for sinners. Colossians 1:13 says, "He has delivered us from the domain of

---

3. Jerome, quoted in Mark W. Elliott, ed., *Old Testament XI - Isaiah 40–66: Ancient Christian Commentary on Scripture* (Downers Grove, IL: InterVarsity Press, 2007), 174.

darkness and transferred us to the kingdom of his beloved Son." In Luke 19:10, Jesus says, "For the Son of Man came to seek and to save the lost." In other words, he came to seek people who can't find their way out of the darkness. Jesus says in Matthew 9:13, "I came not to call the righteous, but sinners." He came to shed light on them. So by believing in the Messiah, gentiles will step out of the darkness. Part of believing is understanding that he came as a Savior to save us from our sin.

> It shall come to pass in the latter days
>> that the mountain of the house of the LORD
> shall be established as the highest of the mountains,
>> and it shall be lifted up above the hills;
> and peoples shall flow to it,
>> and many nations shall come, and say:
> "Come, let us go up to the mountain of the LORD,
>> to the house of the God of Jacob,
> that he may teach us his ways
>> and that we may walk in his paths."
> For out of Zion shall go forth the law,
>> and the word of the LORD from Jerusalem. (Mic 4:1–2)

The prophet Micah was looking forward to the last days when Jerusalem will be exalted. As a result, the gentiles will come and learn the ways of the Lord. There are many references in the New Testament that state the fact that we are living in the latter days (Acts 2:17; 2 Tim 3:1; Heb 1:2; Jas 5:3; 1 Pet 1:20; 2 Pet 3:3; etc.). Thus the prophet was anticipating when Christ shall rule over all the nations and teach them.

The psalmist says, "Who shall ascend the hill of the LORD? And who shall stand in his holy place? He who has clean hands and a pure heart, who does not lift up his soul to what is false and does not swear deceitfully" (Ps 24:3–4). Through the sacrificial work of Christ, people are made pure and enabled to ascend to the holy hill of God.

"For from the rising of the sun to its setting my name will be great among the nations, and in every place incense will be offered to my name, and a pure offering. For my name will be great among the nations, says the LORD of hosts" (Mal 1:11). The prophet Malachi was looking forward to the time when all nations of the earth will worship God in every place. He looked to the time when God will expect worship not only in Jerusalem but in other nations, too. Malachi was looking for the time when all the nations will give a pure offering to the Lord of hosts.

The Old Testament also records a few gentiles who became worshipers of the God of Israel. For example, Rahab was a gentile and known to be a prostitute. Yet she someway found out that the God of Israel is the true God and determined to worship him "for the LORD your God, he is God in the heavens above and on the earth beneath" (Josh 2:11). In fact, Matthew lists Rahab as one of the ancestors of Jesus along with two other gentiles, Tamar and Ruth (Matt 1:3, 5). Rahab is also listed among the great people of faith (Heb 11:31).

The Bible also records the account of Naaman, another gentile and commander of the army of the king of Syria who was healed from his leprosy through the prophet Elisha and became a worshiper of the God of Israel. He asked when returning to his own country, "please let there be given to your servant two mule loads of earth, for from now on your servant will not offer burnt offering or sacrifice to any god but the LORD" (2 Kgs 5:17).

When Jesus was rebuking the scribes and Pharisees, he said "Woe to you, scribes and Pharisees, hypocrites! For you travel across sea and land to make a single proselyte, and when he becomes a proselyte, you make him twice as much a child of hell as yourselves" (Matt 23:15). Gentiles who would become Israelites by being circumcised or by adopting the Jewish culture and practices were known as proselytes. These proselytes were considered to be true Israelites on the merit of following the entire Old Testament law, as well as all the rabbinic instructions. Now one does not need to become an Israelite to be part of the people of God.

The Mystery Hidden for Ages

Along with these passages, I believe other Old Testament passages foretell the salvation of the gentiles (Gen 12:3; 28:14; Pss 22:27–28; 86:9; Isa 2:2–4; 9:2–7; 11:10; 42:1–9; 49:6; 56:6–8; 60:1–3; 66:18–23; Dan 7:14; Amos 9:11–12; etc.). But what was it that the Old Testaments saints could not see fully? We have already noted that the mystery was not something completely new since the Jews understood that gentiles can be saved. They understood that through God's free grace, the gentiles could obtain salvation, but they did not perceive that one day the church would be made up of Jew and gentile, male and female, slave and free, Greek and barbarian, all placed in an equilibrium of perfect impartiality in Christ Jesus (Gal 3:27–28; Col 3:11).

The idea that the gentiles would be fellow heirs, fellow members of the body, and fellow partakers of the promise in Christ Jesus is not stressed in the Old Testament. In other words, the idea that both Jews and gentiles will equally partake of the unsearchable riches of Christ in his body was not perceived by the Old Testament saints. They never understood that Jews and gentiles would literally be one in the body of Christ.

Paul stresses another mystery that the Old Testament saints failed to grasp. Apart from the mystery in Ephesians, we find another mystery in Colossians 1:26–27, "the mystery hidden from ages and generations but now revealed to his saints. To them God chose to make known how great among the Gentiles are the riches of the glory of this mystery, which is Christ in you, the hope of glory." The prophets did not perceive that there would arise an organism formed of Jews and gentiles and that the Messiah would indwell each member of the body. Neither did the Jews understand that a day was coming when God, through the Holy Spirit, would indwell both Jewish and gentile believers.

Why did Paul find it necessary to write to the Ephesians and Colossians about this mystery? Part of the answer is that he wanted to proclaim this revelation that God entrusted to him. But there is more to it. The gentiles were "alienated from the life of God" (Eph 4:18; see also Col 1:21) and from the "commonwealth of Israel and strangers to the covenants of promise" (Eph 2:12). Thus a deep hostility formed between Jews and the gentiles that created a wall of separation. Also, the growing number of the gentiles in the church probably created strife between the Jews and the gentiles.

On the one side was the danger that believing Jews would still boast in their position as people of God and heirs of the covenants of promise, and on the other, the gentiles probably still considered themselves inferior to the Jews because of their former position. Thus Paul found it necessary to remind them all of the mystery of Christ who not only made Jews and gentiles right with each other despite previous religious, racial, and ethnic barriers, but he also brought them to the same level of equality before God.

The Relationship of Israel and the Church

One of the concepts many scholars use to refer to the church is "the people of God." Some have argued that since this concept is used to describe both the New Testament church and the Old Testament Israel, there must be a certain continuity of the church. However, others refute this argument by saying that there is discontinuity of the church since Israel's earthy promises must be fulfilled. How are we to understand the relationship of Israel and the church in light of African traditional religions?

Robert Saucy suggests that we should not come down on the side of a "radical discontinuity."[4] We should also avoid taking a position of *radical continuity*. In other words, the biblical concept of the people of God supports both a certain continuity and discontinuity. G. K. Beale and Benjamin Gladd write,

> Accordingly, an element of discontinuity or "newness" runs through the entire New Testament. Depending on the topic, some elements tend to stand more in continuity with the Old Testament and others seem to be in discontinuity. The New Testament writers, on occasion, tip their hat to this notion of continuity/discontinuity by employing the term *mystery*.[5]

I am much aware of the debated issues about this relationship since "many of the divisions between Christian churches arise from differing ways of understanding this relationship."[6] However, my point in this book is that whichever position one takes, it tends to deny any suggestion of continuity in the African traditional religions. For instance in the argument about continuity and discontinuity, both groups hold the idea of the Old Testament Israelites as the people of God. But nowhere in the Scriptures do we read that other nations were called the people of God. As we will see in chapter 5, none of the other the nations, including the pre-Christian Africans, were the people of God; they were a people "without God in the world" (Eph 2:12).

However, when God called out Abraham to make him a nation, he did not completely abandon other nations. God's end goal in calling Abraham is to redeem other nations for his own glory. All believing gentiles in Christ were "chosen before the foundation of the world" (Eph 1:4).

Made Minister of the Mystery

Paul did not receive this ministry because of his scholastic background since he and his team were "not sufficient in ourselves to claim anything as coming from us, but our sufficiency is from God" (2 Cor 3:5). He received his ministry purely by God's undeserved mercy. Paul says in 2 Corinthians 4:1, "Therefore, having

---

4. Robert Saucy, "Israel and the Church: A Case for Discontinuity," 239–259, quoted in John S. Feinberg, *Continuity and Discontinuity: Perspectives on the Relationship Between the Old and New Testaments* (Wheaton, IL: Crossway, 1988), 239.

5. G. K. Beale and Benjamin L. Gladd, *Hidden but Now Revealed: A Biblical Theology of Mystery* (Downers Grove, IL: InterVarsity Press, 2014), 18, emphasis original.

6. Feinberg, *Continuity and Discontinuity*, 17.

this ministry by the mercy of God, we do not lose heart." Paul suffered many horrific circumstances for the sake of his gospel ministry. In 2 Corinthians 11:23–33 he gives a summary of his suffering – he was imprisoned; he once was stoned; and he spent many days without food and water. Paul went through all kind of suffering, yet he still acknowledged that he received his ministry by God's mercy.

It was sometimes because of his teaching of the mystery of the church that Paul suffered. In fact, he wrote the epistle to the Ephesians when he was imprisoned in Rome (Eph 3:1; 4:1). He was imprisoned for having preached the gospel that asserts that gentiles are fellow heirs in the covenant promise. The Jews persecuted and imprisoned Paul because he was the apostle of the gentiles and preached the gospel to them. But through all of this persecution, he boasted that he was a prisoner of Christ. Though Paul suffered, he recognized the fact that he was owned by Christ. Even during his trials, Paul told the Ephesians, "So I ask you not to lose heart over what I am suffering for you, which is your glory" (Eph 3:13).

Paul considered it a great privilege that among the twelve disciples of Jesus, he was chosen by grace to spread the good news about the mystery of Christ to the gentiles. Under the power and influence of the Holy Spirit, Paul was made a minister who would bring understanding to all about the union of the Jews and gentiles into one organism. This mystery was hidden in God until it was revealed. Paul, who had fiercely persecuted the church, saw it as an underserved gift from God to proclaim the unsearchable riches pertaining to salvation in Christ.

Why Does the Church Exist?

What was God's intent in bringing both Jews and gentiles into one organism, the church? Why did God abolish the ethnic and hostile barrier that once separated gentiles and Jews? Why does the church exist? God's intention is that "through the church the manifold wisdom of God might now be made known to the rulers and authorities in the heavenly places" (Eph 3:10). The mystery of the church was kept secret to everyone in heaven and on earth; angelic and human beings could not perceive it until the time of its revelation.

Since eternity past, God's intention was that through Christ both Jews and gentiles would become co-heirs of God's blessing in the church. The church is such a marvelous manifestation of God's glory through which we know the wisdom of God who works all things according to the counsel of his will. Such an understanding compels us to worship God more. In other words, the church exists for the glory of God since the understanding of this mystery of Christ, displayed in the church, compels both angels and believers to worship God more.

Conclusion

In the previous chapters, we have seen that the unity of the church is one of the greatest themes in the writings of Paul. In fact, a serious study of the New Testament will reveal that every writer points to the unity of believers. We must commit ourselves to the unity of the church. We must not be the agents of division within the body of Christ. It is sinful to separate ourselves into groups that accept and reject others based on their ethnicity or their nationality. Christ's redemptive work on the cross has united us together, and his love compels us to esteem others better than ourselves.

With a united spirit, we have the mind of Christ who thought that being exalted was not something to hold onto, but gave it up to become a servant to those who were in need (Phil 2:5–8). As we move into the next chapters, this is my prayer:

> that according to the riches of his glory he may grant you to be strengthened with power through his Spirit in your inner being, so that Christ may dwell in your hearts through faith – that you, being rooted and grounded in love, may have strength to comprehend with all the saints what is the breadth and length and height and depth, and to know the love of Christ that surpasses knowledge, that you may be filled with all the fullness of God.
>
> Now to him who is able to do far more abundantly than all that we ask or think, according to the power at work within us, to him be glory in the church and in Christ Jesus throughout all generations, forever and ever. Amen. (Eph 3:16–21)

Part 2

The Church in Africa

4

The Concepts of Christ in African Christianity
A Brief Reflection on the Christology of John Mbiti and Kwame Bediako

Engaging the African Culture

Over the last few decades, many African countries have known massive migratory movements as a result of ethnic conflicts, wars, and unemployment. As people migrate to more peaceful countries within Africa, the almost sudden presence of displaced people creates a multicultural society and cultural pluralism. This cultural pluralism is basically created out of insecurity as both the host citizens and displaced people fear losing their distinctive cultural identities. While trying to be authentic to their cultural or religious identity, the host countries still experience a decrease in religious homogeneity. This phenomenon leads to an increase of religious pluralism which in turn challenges churches to communicate the Christian faith.

Since the church is an interface or point of contact between the Christian faith and the culture, churches must to be alert to the need to give a theological translation that connects up with where people are currently in their culture. In chapter 2, we emphasized that translation is more than simply finding the best word for a Greek or Hebrew word. It's about unpacking a word and explaining the concepts it represents in ways that make sense to the people where they are in their culture.

For instance, anyone who is familiar with stones will intuitively understand that the psalmist's words "the LORD is my rock" (Ps 18:2) do not imply that God is made of stones or that he is being weather-beaten by wind. Rather, the metaphor evokes the idea of being protected. A rock is a place of stability and safety. In the same way, God is a safe place on which we can stand and be secure. "The LORD is my shepherd" (Ps 23:1) is similar language that depicts the idea of protection using imagery that can be easily understood, a shepherd of a flock.

There is a real danger that we may use Christian terminology which Christian congregations don't understand, for example justification, substitutionary atonement, reconciliation, etc. We need to translate such words into language that connects the ideas they communicate to people where they are. How do we best explain these words? We need to show how these words connect up with our culture, not only to give synonyms of the words but also translating them into language and actions that are understandable in the culture. John S. Mbiti explains translation this way:

> We cannot effectively carry out mission in a foreign language. Just as missionaries from overseas had to learn our language, so must we put mission in a language which makes sense to those whom we missionize. In other words, we have to sing the Gospel in our tunes, set to our music, played on our instruments. I speak metaphorically. We must drum it out with our great drums, on our tom-toms, on our waist-shaped drums, for only these can vibrate and awaken entire villages: the violin is too feeble to awaken the sleeping pagans of our society. This applies equally in Africa as it does in Europe and America where the Gospel must be sung aloud.[1]

Based on what Mbiti says, I believe there is a need today to communicate the Christian faith in light of the challenges we face from African traditional religions. Reaching the African community and making sure the biblical truth is understood as what it really is must be the work of the church in Africa. How should we communicate the Christian faith to a society that has been built on traditional beliefs? How can we translate the key ideas of the Christian doctrine into a language our pluralistic culture can understand? In what sense are African forms of expression able to communicate understanding of Christ?

Our work as the church will be effective if we communicate or translate the gospel into a vernacular which is clear to an *unschooled* African. But as we do so, let us be careful not to mishandle the truth of the Bible. Contextualization demands that we effectively understand both the culture and our theology. In fact when we grasp the meaning of our theology, we will be able to

---

1. John S. Mbiti, *The Crisis of Mission in Africa* (Mukono: Uganda Church Press, 1971), 5.

communicate it effectively to our culture. C. S. Lewis writes, "I have come to the conviction that if you cannot translate your thoughts into uneducated language, then your thoughts were confused. Power to translate is the test of having really understood one's own meaning. A passage from some theological work for translation into the vernacular ought to be a compulsory paper in every Ordination examination."[2]

Lewis introduces a very important element to what Mbiti has just said. There is a need to speak the gospel truth in the language that Africans must understand, but we should also think correctly about our Christian faith. In other words, what story can we tell or analogies can we use to communicate what the gospel is all about? Lewis suggests that part of the value in translating our Christian faith "is the test of having really understood one's own meaning," to have a clear theological view of the gospel.

Most African theologians have contributed a lot in communicating the Christian faith and the African traditional religions. They have made a remarkable impact by helping us to think properly about the Christian faith in relation to our African culture. However in trying to explain the biblical truth in light of African traditional religions, some have sidetracked the main themes of the Christian faith. In this chapter, I am going to open up a discussion among massive discussions that we will never exhaust on these few pages. What I can do is try to map out the idea of Christ and to raise an objection to the debated issue of continuity and discontinuity in the understanding of God in Africa, which is for me an area of interest. I will gladly tell you what I think the Bible says but also try to create space for you to think through what you think. In other words, I will try to open up a discussion on the idea of Christ in Africa for further thoughts. But let us try to set everything in context before we take this discussion further.

The Jesus of John Mbiti

Here in the second part of this book, I will try to reflect a little bit on the question of John Mbiti's understanding of Christ. In this chapter, I try to draw a distinction between what I consider to be the narrowed arguments of John Mbiti on Christology and the rather more deeply engaging arguments of the apostle Paul. Let's begin by trying to frame the issue. John Mbiti says,

2. C. S. Lewis, "Christian Apologetics" [1945], in *God in the Dock: Essays on Theology and Ethics* (Grand Rapids: Eerdmans, 1970), 96.

> God the Father of our Lord Jesus Christ is the same God who for
> thousands of years has been known and worshipped in various
> ways within the religious life of African peoples. . . . *[He]* was not
> a stranger in Africa prior to the coming of missionaries. . . . the
> Gospel enabled people to utter the name of Jesus Christ . . . that
> final and completing element that crowns traditional religiosity
> and brings its flickering light to full brilliance.[3]

Of course this is Mbiti's opinion, although it leaves me slightly
uncomfortable. I am not going to follow this point through any further, not
because I am unconcerned about this debate, but because I want to note the
general points that it raises. Mbiti's argument seems to me to raise a point that
we cannot really get away from.

Mbiti is moving in a direction which you and I may describe as "Christianity
without the biblical Christ." On the one hand, he is trying to make the point
that the God of Scripture is the same God worshipped in the pre-Christian
era in Africa. On the other hand, Mbiti asserts that Christ came to complete
an element that was missing in African traditional religions. According to
Mbiti, Christ does not negate African traditional religions but crowns them.

I am going to develop this discussion by looking specifically at the apostle
Paul who opens up a helpful way. He takes things in a very different direction.
We will interact with his writings and see how we can understand the idea of
Christ in light of African traditional religions. This discussion between Mbiti
and the apostle Paul illustrates very well the key questions that lie behind this
chapter: How do we perceive Christ in light of African traditional religions?
Did Christ's work of salvation abolish African traditional religions? And is
there such a thing as African Christianity?

One of the fundamental points to make is that the apostle Paul explains
both the godlessness of pre-Christian Africans and Christ as the unique
revelation of God. The point I am making here is that to claim that the God
of Scripture is the same God worshiped in the pre-Christian era in Africa is
profanity. All pre-Christ Africans were idolaters like other gentiles of the past.
The question is how do we come to such an understanding?

---

3. John Mbiti quoted in Kwame Bediako, *Theology and Identity: The Impact of Culture upon Christian Thought in the Second Century and in Modern Africa* (Oxford: Regnum, 1999), 331.

The Africanization of Jesus by Kwame Bediako

In 2000, Kwame Bediako wrote *Jesus in Africa* that sought to examine the understanding of Jesus in the African approach. The book deserves thorough discussions, but in this chapter, I limit my comments to some points he made. In my opinion, Bediako's book sounds the alarm about the tendency to Africanize Christ. Not only has Bediako seemed to strengthen Mbiti's argument on the continuity of the understanding of God in African traditional religions, but also Mbiti's understanding of Christ. Bediako writes, "In contrast to what has happened in the earlier evangelization of Europe, in Africa, the God whose name had been hallowed in indigenous languages in the pre-Christian tradition was found to be the God of the Bible, in a way that neither Zeus, nor Jupiter, nor Odin could be."[4]

Bediako claims that the God of the Bible preceded the missionaries who brought the gospel in Africa in the sense that God was already known and worshiped in the pre-Christian era. But I have mixed feelings about this argument. On the one hand, I agree that Africans had the idea of a divine being. On the other hand, I still insist that the God of the Bible was not known to pre-Christian minds since the Bible, as we will see, strongly disproves such continuity.

Bediako does not stop there. His book *Theology and Identity* sounds another alarm on the understanding of the person and work of Christ. Bediako treats Christ under the category of ancestor, "thus deviating himself from the biblical concept of Christ as one being with God, the Father, as opposed to ancestors."[5] He also states that Christ was already at work in African traditional religions. Bediako argues that the missionaries failed to grasp the universal activity and nature of Christ. He writes,

> Because of the modern missionary misapprehension on this specific point of universality, fundamental questions on the possible positive meaning of Christ for the pre-Christian religious past could hardly surface or be taken with sufficient seriousness in the missionary era. The New Testament, on the other hand, shows an awareness of the problem, and significantly, approaches a solution not from the standpoint of the nearness or otherwise

---

4. Kwame Bediako, *Jesus in Africa: The Christian Gospel in African History and Experience* (Akropong-Akuapem, Ghana: Regnum Africa, 2000), 16–17.

5. Christopher Magezi and Jacob T. Igba, "African Theology and African Christology: Difficulty and Complexity in Contemporary Definitions and Methodological Frameworks," *Theological Studies* 74, no. 1 (2018). https://hts.org.za/index.php/hts/article/view/4590.

of the Gentile religious heritage to the more "enlightened" Jewish tradition, but rather on the basis of the universality of Jesus Christ.[6]

Bediako seems to affirm Mbiti's arguments on both the theology of God and of Christ. They both assert that there is some positive in African traditional religions. From their stand, it is so easy to conclude that Christianity in Africa is rooted in African traditional religions. Kwame Bediako, Bolaji Idowu, John Mbiti, and other African scholars may defend with particulars the positivity of African traditional religions, but there is a long and consistent defense of the centrality of Christ by the apostle Paul which we cannot get away from. D. A. Carson is right in his comment on Hebrews 1:1:

> In the past, God spoke: he has always been a talking God. But in these last days – the eschatological framework is inescapable – his final "Word," as it were, is his Son, Jesus Christ. . . . If this is true, to ignore him or to treat him as one option among many is to defy God our Maker and Judge. And one day we shall give an account to him.[7]

The Continuity of the Understanding of God in Africa

Through their writings, Bediako, Idowu, and Mbiti have sought to identify a continuity of African traditional religions and the Christian faith. They have identified points of contact between the Christian faith and African traditional religions arguing that the God of the Bible is the same God Africans used to worship before the missionaries came to Africa. In other words, they all argue that the God the missionaries sought to proclaim through the gospel was already being worshiped in Africa.

Idowu considered the key aspect of religion to be the understanding of who God is: "The uniqueness of each religion lies in its conception of Deity and its apprehension of the divine will. Here is the heart of every religion, its essential theology and the motive of its ethical emphasis."[8] Moreover, he assumes that the being worshiped in Africa before the Christian missionary enterprise shares the same fundamental identity with the true God, saying

---

6. Bediako, *Theology and Identity*, 247.

7. D. A. Carson, *The Gagging of God: Christianity Confronts Pluralism* (Grand Rapids: Zondervan, 1996), 345.

8. Idowu, "Faiths in Interaction," *Orita: Ibadan Journal of Religious Studies* 4, no. 2 (Dec 1970): 94.

"Africa recognizes only one God, the Supreme, Universal God . . . one and the same God, the Creator of all the ends of the earth."[9]

Elsewhere, Bediako agrees that, "In saying 'God,' Idowu means 'God as revealed in the Biblical religion' and who 'so loved the world that he sent his only begotten Son to redeem' it. But, for Idowu, 'God' also means Olodumare, God as known and experienced in Yoruba pre-Christian religious tradition."[10]

I think the continuity of God is a point that we cannot really get away from since it has been a question of debate among many African theologians. Bediako is really trying to highlight this point by showing that there is no intrinsic difference between the God of African traditional religions and the revealed God of the Scriptures. Furthermore, Mbiti has written two popular books, *Concepts of God in Africa* and *African Religions and Philosophy*, in which he brings out the same idea of the continuity of God by establishing the attributes of God.[11]

However, in order to affirm or to disapprove the continuity of God, we must read or understand African traditional religions through the lenses of the revealed biblical truth about God and not the other way round. In other words, we should let our biblical theology dictate our interpretation of every religion, including African traditional religions.

A Pauline Approach to Christ

It is not my intention to negate the study of African traditional religions. Such an idea might destroy the bridges that carry the gospel to the African culture. I totally agree with Bediako when he says, "Many Africans gained access to the original sources of Christian revelation as mediated through African traditional religious terminology and ideas."[12] But I believe that the apostle Paul gives us straightforward answers on understanding of the continuity of God and understanding Christ. At this junction, I will let Paul lead the discussion. To do so, let us take a journey into some of his epistles. Parallel to Paul's epistles, we will also have a glimpse at the Gospels.

---

9. Idowu, "The Study of Religion, with Special Reference to African Traditional Religion," *Orita: Ibadan Journal of Religious Studies* 1, no. 1 (Jun 1957): 12.

10. Bediako, *Theology and Identity*, 279.

11. John S. Mbiti, *Concepts of God in Africa* (London: SPCK, 1970); and John S. Mbiti, *African Religions and Philosophy* (Nairobi: Heinemann Kenya, 1969).

12. Bediako, *Jesus in Africa*, 17.

General Revelation

When God reveals himself, he reveals himself according to his own character or nature. Theology is our attempt to understand the truth that God has revealed about himself. In the Christian faith, biblical theology is not based upon someone's speculative philosophy but according to the Holy Scriptures that must be believed under the illumination of the Holy Spirit.

Theologians have tried to distinguish between two sorts of revelation: general revelation and special revelation. General revelation is the knowledge of God given to every human being, without any distinction, through creation and through the written law on hearts. The idea of general revelation is based upon two texts of Scriptures: Romans 1:19–20, "For what can be known about God is plain to them, because God has shown it to them. For his invisible attributes, namely, his eternal power and divine nature, have been clearly perceived, ever since the creation of the world, in the things that have been made. So they are without excuse"; and Romans 2:15, "They show that the work of the law is written on their hearts, while their conscience also bears witness, and their conflicting thoughts accuse or even excuse them."

These passages point us to the reality that God has not hidden his revelation from all people who have ever lived on earth. Paul stresses the idea that the creation serves as a medium of God's revelation. God is not hidden in every created thing we perceive, but through them we can see the Creator God. In other words, every created thing tells us of the God who is the author of everything seen and unseen. So we must assert that even the most atheistic person on earth has a sense of divinity. No one is exempt from this reality. God has revealed himself to everyone across all ages and on every continent, which explains why Africans were religious in the pre-Christian era. John Calvin explains this idea more clearly,

> Therefore, since from the beginning of the world no country, town or even household has managed to do without religion, there we have a tacit admission that in the heart of every human being is stamped a feeling for divinity. Idolatry itself gives abundant proof of this idea. For we know how far man contrives to abase himself, however reluctantly, and how ready he is to honor other creatures in preference to himself.[13]

---

13. John Calvin, *Institutes of the Christian Religion*, translated from the first French edition of 1541 by Robert White (Edinburgh: Banner of Truth, 2014), 4.

According to Calvin, the reason there is a plurality of religions in the world is the fact that deep within the adherents of these religions lies a thirst for the divine. Human beings have a deep longing for a transcendent being who can give meaning to their existence in this vast universe. Or to put it in simple words, human beings were created religious. Gehman affirms that "the evidence worldwide from all the peoples is overwhelming. Man is not a religious animal with religious cults everywhere that have evolved over time. A knowledge and belief in God or divinities is found in every continent and virtually in every corner of our globe. To be sure, we also find universal evidence of man's attempt to escape from God and replace him with substitute idols."[14] Thus Calvin calls idolatry the worship of an assumed God.

Paul continues in Romans 1:21–23, "Although they knew God, they did not honor him as God or give thanks to him, but they became futile in their thinking, and their foolish hearts were darkened. Claiming to be wise, they became fools, and exchanged the glory of the immortal God for images resembling mortal man and birds and animals and creeping things." Paul argues that even though God can be known through the created world, people, namely gentiles, fail to worship him for who he is and to do his will. The question that is often asked is this: Was Paul talking about all the gentiles in general when he used the pronoun "they"? The right answer is yes. Paul wrote the book of Romans to point out that the gentiles and Jews are at the same level of human inability to worship God. Paul wanted to show how these two groups have all it takes to know God. Unfortunately, they fail to worship him in light of what they know about him through creation and conscience.

Unless there are some biblical proofs that African traditional religions came from the Jewish religion, we cannot say that the God who was worshiped by pre-Christian Africans is the same as the God of the Scriptures since Africans are part of the gentiles described by Paul. Even though assumptions about the God that Africans worshiped are close to the attributes of the God revealed in the Scripture, there is no way to conclude that he is "intrinsically"[15] the same God.

I believe that the assumptions about the attributes of God in African traditional religions that John Mbiti came up with in his book *Concepts of God in Africa*[16] were the result of general revelation as described in Romans 1.

---

14. Richard J. Gehman, *African Traditional Religion in Biblical Perspective – Revised Edition* (Nairobi: East African Educational Publishers, 2005), 346.

15. Bediako, *Theology and Identity*, 270.

16. Mbiti, *Concepts of God in Africa*.

But these assumptions had no impact in leading Africans to worship the true God since, "None is righteous, no, not one; no one understands; no one seeks God. All have turned aside; together they have become worthless; no one does good, not even one" (Rom 3:10–12). Byang Kato writes,

> Idolatry is evidently a part of African traditional religions. . . . It is unrealistic to deny that idol worship is part of African traditional religions. . . . while it is true that the worshipper looks beyond the wood and stone, the emptiness of his practice amounts to idolatry. He can be said to bow down to wood and stone.[17]

If the Bible affirms that "no one understands; no one seeks for God," then our knowledge of God is erroneous somewhere because true knowledge of God leads to worshiping him. Thus even our African traditional religions is among the religions that practice idolatry, which we are to call a worldly religion. Knowing some attributes of God does not equate with knowledge of the true God. Every assumption we might have concerning God apart from the Scripture is a result of that awareness of God which he has written on our hearts (Rom 2:15).

Christ Is the Perfect Special Revelation of God

General revelation is not too weak to reveal God to Africans. Neither is the written law on their hearts too feeble to do the work. But it is our fallenness that has made us unable to worship God as he is. Furthermore, general revelation does not reveal the salvation plan of God. It cannot save sinners from the wrath to come. Thus it is God's righteousness that brings us true knowledge of him. We only know God and worship him through Christ who is the revelation of God. Paul writes, "For God, who said, 'Let light shine out of darkness,' has shone in our hearts to give the light of the knowledge of the glory of God in the face of Jesus Christ" (2 Cor 4:6).

Without Christ, it was not possible for African traditional religions to come to the knowledge of God. Through Christ's revelation, we not only come to the knowledge of God but we also discover who we are. Our true nature is revealed. This is what Moses expressed when he said, "You have set our iniquities before you, our secret sins in the light of your presence" (Ps 90:8). This is also what the prophet Isaiah experienced when he saw God on his throne and heard the angels say, "Holy, Holy, Holy is the LORD of hosts; the whole earth is full of

---

17. Byang H. Kato, *Theological Pitfalls in Africa* (Kisumu, Kenya: Evangel, 1975), 20.

his glory!" (Isa 6:1–3). And Isaiah said, "Woe is me! For I am lost; for I am a man of unclean lips, and I dwell in the midst of a people of unclean lips"; then he added these terrifying words, "for my eyes have seen the King, the LORD of hosts!" (6:5). In the same way, the deeper we go in knowledge of the Lord through Christ, the more we are going to see what sins are in our lives. The nearer we get to God, the more we will see what we really are. Alister McGrath writes, "One of the central points made by Christian theologians is that light shows up things as they really are, dispelling illusions. Illumination allows a reality check, forcing us to confront what are at times some awkward truths."[18]

If the eyes of our understanding are truly enlightened, the first thing we learn is the truth about ourselves. This means that we realize that we are all hopeless, we are all lost, we are all damned, we are all sinners – every one of us. "None is righteous, no, not one" (Rom 3:10). People who see this will stop boasting about their religiosity immediately. They will not boast about their morality, the goodness of their traditions, their good works, their good deeds, their knowledge, their learning, or anything else. It is the gospel alone that gives this understanding; nothing else can. The gospel reduces us to the same level, every one of us. It is the Spirit alone who can bring a person to this point.

I believe this is one of the reasons why believers are greatly encouraged to attend church: to listen to the word of God and to read their Bibles. The Bible is God's book; it is the special revelation of God. The message of the Bible from beginning to end is designed to bring us back to God, to humble us before God, and to enable us to see our true relationship to him. Martyn Lloyd-Jones puts it this way: "The Bible is not an ordinary book – it is God's Book, and it is a Book about God and man's relationship to him. Therefore, every time we consider or study the Bible we are, of necessity, worshipping."[19]

As the Scriptures remind us in Matthew 5:13–16, we Christians are set as lights in the world, as the salt of society, and like a city set upon a hill. Of course, we are not the light of the world in the same sense that Christ is. When light refers to Christ, it is describing him as Savior and not merely as one who reveals great truths. Christians have just been illuminated by the light that is Christ, who dwells within them. William Hendriksen says,

> Christians are never a light in and by themselves. They are light
> "in the Lord" (Eph 5:8). Christ is the true, the original "light of the

---

18. Alister McGrath, *Christian Belief for Everyone: Book One: Faith and the Creeds* (London: SPCK, 2013), 35.

19. Martyn Lloyd-Jones, *Romans: Exposition of Chapter 1 – The Gospel of God* (Edinburgh: Banner of Truth, 1985), 1.

world." . . . Believers are "the light of the world" in a secondary or derived sense. He is "the light lighting" (John 1:9). They are the light lighted. He is the sun. They resemble the moon, reflecting the sun's light. Apart from Christ they cannot shine . . . as long as Christ's followers remain in living contact with the original light they are a light to others (cf. John 15:4, 5).[20]

When Christians are called the light of the world, there is clearly no saving significance in the description; we do not accomplish salvation. But we do point it out. It is our function to live as redeemed people. We are to show the quality of life properly to the people of God and in this way act as light to all people. We are to point the people of this darkened world to Christ the Savior and Light of the world.

Jesus Christ took risks to heal the most infirm, to defend the most excluded, and to retrieve the unrecoverable. This work cost him his honor and his life. He lost his face to give us a face. And near the end, he said this prayer for his disciples then and now,

> I do not ask that you take them out of the world, but that you keep them from the evil one. They are not of the world, just as I am not of the world. Sanctify them in the truth; your word is truth. As you sent me into the world, so I have sent them into the world. And for their sake I consecrate myself, that they also may be sanctified in truth. (John 17:15–19)

As the church of God, we are to reveal Christ in this darkened world. To be born again is to be chosen to bear witness about Jesus Christ, the Savior, to this world. Christ is the only hope to the world today; above him there is no other hope! A. W. Tozer writes,

> This blessed knowledge is not given to be enjoyed selfishly. The more perfectly we know God the more we will feel the desire to translate the new-found knowledge into deeds of mercy toward suffering humanity. The God who gave all to us will continue to give all through us as we come to know Him better. . . . any intensified knowledge of God will soon begin to affect those around us in the Christian community. And we must seek purposefully to share our increasing light with fellow members of the household of God.

---

20. William Hendriksen, *Matthew: New Testament Commentary* (Edinburgh: Banner of Truth, 1974), 284.

This we can best do by keeping the majesty of God in full focus in all our public services.[21]

Is Christ Really a Redeemer of African Heritage?

In his book *Theology and Identity*, Bediako spends a few pages supporting Mbiti's argument on Christ as the redeemer of African heritage. A central point Bediako tries to make is the universal nature and activity of Christ among the heathen, namely the gentiles in the pre-Christian as well as the post-Christian eras.

Unfortunately, Mbiti's idea that "Christ brought the flickering light of the African traditional religion to full brilliance"[22] lessens the gravity of our alienation from God and the sense that we are lost in sin and misery. This idea also reduces Christ's work on the cross. In this declaration, Mbiti and Bediako are reading the Bible through the lenses of African traditional religions and not the other way round. Their understanding of Christ and his works violates the authority of Scripture. We are to read every religion through the lenses of Scripture. Daniel Strange writes,

> Scripture often attests to an extreme opposition of "antithesis" within humanity, a conflictual relationship between those who have "truth faith" in this God, and those who have "false faith." This false faith amounts to believing "lies" about this God. Consequently and again mentioned previously, despite the plethora of worldviews and religions that exists in the world, in reality there are only two: those rooted and built up in Christ, and those founded on "hollow and deceptive philosophy, which depends on human tradition and the elemental spiritual forces of this world rather than on Christ" (Col 2:6–10).[23]

When declaring the preeminence of Christ, Paul writes, "He has delivered us from the domain of darkness and transferred us to the kingdom of his beloved Son, in whom we have redemption, the forgiveness of sins. He is the image of the invisible God, the firstborn of all creation" (Col 1:13–15).

---

21. A. W. Tozer, *The Knowledge of the Holy: The Attributes of God, Their Meaning in the Christian Life* (San Francisco: Harper Collins, 1961), 116–117.

22. John Mbiti quoted in Kwame Bediako, *Theology and Identity*, 331.

23. Daniel Strange, *Their Rock Is Not Like Our Rock: A Theology of Religions* (Grand Rapids: Zondervan Academic, 2015), 240.

As Africans, we were separated from Christ before the first missionaries came to our continent, and we had no hope and were without God like the rest of the gentiles (Eph 2:12). We were living in ignorance of God; we had no God in relation to the Jews. We were in total darkness, defilement, guilt, bondage, and misery that took hold of our minds. Even though God left evidence of his handiwork and character in creation in Africa, we are not able to grasp his will because of our darkened minds.

Through his redemptive work, Christ transfers us from our ignorance of God into the full light where not only our sins are swept away but also where we come to the knowledge of God. The knowledge of God comes to us through our encounter with the crucified and risen Christ. Paul writes, "And if Christ has not been raised, your faith is futile and you are still in your sins" (1 Cor 15:17). The work of Christ can never be properly understood apart from understanding his person.

On the one hand, Jesus Christ is described in Colossians 1:15 as "the image of the invisible God." "Image" carries with it at least two ideas. First, it conveys the thought that the Lord Jesus has enabled us to see what God is like. God is Spirit and is, therefore, invisible. But in the person of Christ, God made himself visible to mortal eyes. In that sense, the Lord Jesus is the image of the invisible God. As Jesus said, "Whoever has seen me has seen the Father" (John 14:9). But the word image also conveys the idea of "representative." God originally placed Adam on the earth to represent his interests, but Adam failed. Therefore, God sent his only begotten Son into the world as his representative to care for his interests and to reveal his love to people; in that sense, he is the image of God.[24]

On the other hand, Jesus Christ is described as "the firstborn of all creation" (Col 1:15). The expression "firstborn of all creation" has nothing to do with birth order. It simply means that Christ is God's Son in an eternal relationship. It is a title of priority of position. Jesus Christ existed before all creation and occupies a position of supremacy over it. He is the head and source of creation; he is the fountain of life for every moving creature. So from Colossians 1:16, we understand that Jesus Christ is first in all things, to be listened to, loved, and worshiped by all human beings.

---

24. See the helpful discussion in G. K. Beale, *The Temple and the Church's Mission: A Biblical Theology of the Dwelling Place of God*, NSBT 17 (Downers Grove, IL: InterVarsity Press, 2004), chap. 3.

Conclusion

In his book *African Religions and Philosophy*, Mbiti writes, "African traditional religions are a reality which calls for academic scrutiny and which must be reckoned with in modern fields of life. . . . to ignore these traditional beliefs, attitudes and practices can only lead to a lack of understanding African behavior and problems. Religion is the strongest element in traditional background, and exerts probably the greatest influence upon the thinking and living of the people concerned."[25] Frankly, it is of great importance to study African traditional religions since apologetics demands that we understand both camps: theology and culture. In this sense, negating African traditional religions is creating cultural barriers for the gospel. But we should be very careful not to read Scripture through the eyes of African traditional religions since the Bible is the authority by which we should judge all religions.

Thus in this chapter it was my intention to show that African traditional religions should be counted among other worldly religions like Islam, Hinduism, etc. To claim that the God of Scripture is the same God worshiped in the pre-Christian era in Africa is profanity. All pre-Christ Africans were idolaters like other gentiles of the past. Time and again, Deuteronomy warns the people of God to be careful to follow all that the Lord has commanded and to avoid entanglements, including marriage, with the surrounding peoples for fear of worshiping their gods (Deut 12:29–30). Byang Kato helps us conclude this chapter:

> The knowledge of God through nature and conscience is evidenced by the fact that man has shown interest in religion per se. But his worship has only proved that man has turned to the worship of creation rather than the Creator. While it may be rightly claimed that the new revelation in Christ has not been discontinuous in the sense of God's general revelation, it must be added unequivocally that it is also discontinuous. Redemptive salvation of Christ, first prefigured in the Old Testament, is a new thing. Thus Christ is the fulfillment of the Old Testament and of the deep spiritual need of the human hearts, *but He is not the fulfillment of African traditional religions or any other non-Christian religion.*[26]

There is no continuity of the understanding of God between the Bible and African traditional religions; instead it is my conviction that continuity

---

25. Mbiti, *African Religions and Philosophy*, 1.
26. Kato, *Theological Pitfalls in Africa*, 155. Emphasis original.

may be traced in the pre-Christian Jewish religion. Pre-Christian Africans, like any other gentiles of the past, needed Christ who has borne the wrath of God that is against all unrighteousness (Rom 1:18). God's wrath and curse was directed against Christ so that all elect gentiles "who once were far off" might be "brought near by the blood of Christ" (Eph 2:13). Daniel Strange is right to say, "It is the person and work of Christ that distinguishes Christianity from all other 'faiths' and gives Christianity its exclusive or particular claims."[27]

---

27. Strange, *Their Rock Is Not Like Our Rock*, 245.

5

Corporate Unity in Christ and Its Consequences in Africa
Ephesians 2:11–17

In their book *International Relations*, Joshua Goldstein and Jon Pevehouse discuss six types of international conflicts: ethnic, religious, ideologic, territorial, governmental, and economic.[1] The first three are conflicts over ideas, and the last three are conflicts over interests. Since it is not possible to cover all types of conflicts, I will only focus on ethnic conflicts within the African church. My purpose in this chapter is to prove that our union with Christ is the only weapon that can destroy the dividing walls of hostility between ethnic groups in Africa.

David Tarus has written a book that seeks to present Christian theological responses to ethnopolitical conflicts in Kenya. *A Different Way of Being*[2] sheds more light on understanding intertribal conflicts and how the church should biblically respond with theological perspectives. However, I will not follow through on that path. I will limit my thoughts to African believers' union with Christ despite their ethnic differences within the African church as a whole, which "transcends ethnic divisions."[3] I will also not focus on any ethnic group or any nation as my case study.

---

1. Joshua S. Goldstein and Jon C. Pevehouse, *International Relations: Brief Fourth Edition* (New York: Pearson Longman, 2008).

2. David Tarus, *A Different Way of Being: Towards a Reformed Theology of Ethnopolitical Cohesion for the Kenyan Context* (Carlisle, UK: Langham Monographs, 2019).

3. Tarus, *Different Way of Being*, 15.

Defining Ethnicity

Our age seems to be increasingly characterized by division, tribalism, conflict, etc. Unfortunately, these traits are found even among believers. There are growing indications and awareness that the problems are much greater and more frightening than we realize. Unfortunately, most of us are our own greatest problem. These issues are indications that the gospel has not really penetrated to the core of many believers of Christ. For instance, the numerous wars now occurring in central Africa are caused by ethnic conflicts. Goldstein and Pevehouse explain the causes of ethnic conflicts in these words,

> Ethnocentrism, or in-groups bias, is the tendency to see one's own groups in favorable terms and an out-group in unfavorable terms. In-groups biases are stronger when the other group looks different, speaks a different language, or worship in a different way (or all three). All too easily, an out-group can be dehumanized and stripped of all human rights. This dehumanization includes the common use of animal names – "pigs," "dogs," and so forth – for members of the out-group.[4]

Scholars in anthropology have defined "ethnicity" in different ways. The first entry of the Oxford dictionary defines ethnicity as the fact of belonging to a particular race. However, David Kirwa defines ethnicity as the "subjective perception or the phenomenon of belonging to a particular ethnic group";[5] whereas ethnic groups are large groups of people who share ancestral, language, cultural, or religious bonds and a common identity.

Most of the time, conflicts between ethnic groups have substantial aspects; ethnic conflict itself implicates a dislike or hatred that members of one ethnic group feel toward another ethnic group. Incidentally, "ethnic conflict is based not on tangible causes (what someone does) but on intangible ones (who someone is)."[6] Thus if ethnic conflict is based on intangible causes, like the identity of a person, then we should look beyond cultural identity to spiritual identity. This spiritual identity leads us to define the nature of human beings.

---

4. Goldstein and Pevehouse, *International Relations*, 123.

5. Tarus, *Different Way of Being*, 4.

6. Goldstein and Pevehouse, *International Relations*, 120.

Cause of Ethnic Hostility

In his book *Social Contract and Discourses*, Jean-Jacques Rousseau conceives of human beings in the state of nature as innocent, and he suggests that the evil found in a society is social in origin. For Rousseau, we are controlled by social conditions. If you change these conditions, the people will change, too.[7] However, I do not agree with Rousseau. For instance, ethnic conflicts or wars are not only caused by what people of one ethnic group do to others in another group. Causes of these conflicts go beyond actions, as we will see.

Some have suggested that education over time can overcome hostilities between ethnic groups. There is some truth in this. However, even seemingly educated nations have gone through major ethnic conflicts. You and I may probably identify ourselves with the words of the atheist philosopher Bertrand Russell, "Man is a rational animal. So at least we have been told. Throughout a long life I have searched diligently for evidence in favor of this statement. So far, I have not had the good fortune to come across it."[8]

In making this observation, Russell was looking closely at humanity and concluded that most of the time, human actions seem irrational in contrast to the popular belief that a human being is a rational animal. No matter how rational we may think ourselves to be, our actions prove to be irrational in relation to God's absolute morality. Reason cannot unpluck the real cause of ethnic conflicts, which is the sinful heart of human beings. So I suggest that sin is the main root of all ethnic conflicts.

Unity and Peace in Christ

In chapter 2 of this volume, we stated that one of the predominant themes in Ephesians is love. We emphasized that one of the great marks of the body of Christ is the love that Christ is poured into the hearts of believers so that this love can flow through them since "no union can be truly successful unless love is its basis and mode of operation."[9] How then does this idea of believers' union with Christ solve the key issues that Africa faces: division in the church, tribalism, corruption, etc.? John Mbiti expands on the subject this way:

---

7. Jean-Jacques Rousseau, *Social Contract and Discourses*, translated by G. D. H. Cole (Hawthorne, CA: BN Publishing, 2007).

8. Bertrand Russell, *Unpopular Essays* (London: Unwin Brothers, 1921), 95.

9. Harold W. Hoehner, *Ephesians: An Exegetical Commentary* (Grand Rapids: Baker Academic, 2002), 351.

> One of the areas of great absurdity and shame is the matter of
> Church disunity in Africa. Every type of faction and division is to
> be found in our continent. Everybody who wants to start business
> in Church divisions can do so in Africa. Until we put this right
> our mission task will forever be weak and ineffective. . . . Divided
> Christianity has no place in Africa where we are fighting to remove
> the divisions of racialism, tribalism, political parties, and foreign
> political rule. . . . and the main grounds for keeping divisions are
> pride, prejudice, fear and self-interests.[10]

Since we Africans are part of the elements of the mystery of the church,
how does this contribute to solving our sociological problems – corruption,
tribalism, racialism, division, etc.? What can we learn about African practices
and beliefs in light of believers' union with Christ? Believers from different
countries and from different tribes within a given country need one another.
And this is what the apostle Paul expresses in the second chapter of the book
of Ephesians.

In the previous chapter, we began the discussion of godlessness in the
pre-Christian era. There I argue that like any other group of gentiles, Africans
were not worshiping the true God. In the pre-Christian era, we were all pagans
dwelling in the darkness of our sins and in the shadow of death, seeking to
please our sinful nature while opposing God. In as much as we may defend
our African traditional religions and the good things we perceive in them, we
can never overlook the biblical truth about gentiles. Gentiles live according
to the standards of the flesh.

In fact, Paul says we were all dead in our trespasses and sins (Eph 2:1).
This means our entire nature, our sense and reason, was debased and tending
towards ungodliness and vice. We were not half dead; we were not injured;
but we could not breathe spiritually. Our spirits were completely dead, not
fainted, in sins. Furthermore, we "were at that time separated from Christ,
alienated from the commonwealth of Israel and strangers to the covenants
of promise" (Eph 2:12). Thus we might conclude that "human beings do not
merely commit sins. They are in bondage to sin, so that sin rules over them.
Paul remarks that 'sin reigned in death' (Rom 5:21). Death here refers to both
spiritual death – separation from God – and physical death."[11]

---

10. John S. Mbiti, *The Crisis of Mission in Africa* (Mukono: Uganda Church Press, 1971), 5.

11. Thomas Schreiner, *New Testament Theology: Magnifying God in Christ* (Grand Rapids: Baker Academic, 2008), 534.

Uncircumcised

In the book of Ephesians, Paul is reminding the believing gentiles to remember their former position vis-à-vis Christ: "Therefore remember that at one time you Gentiles in the flesh, called 'the uncircumcision' by what is called the circumcision, which is made in the flesh by hands" (Eph 2:11). In contrast to Jews who were gentiles in heart, Paul wanted gentiles to remember that their condition was even worse since they didn't have certain privileges that Jews had. Gentiles were not bearing the covenant sign in their flesh. Consequently, they were separated from the covenants of promise (2:12). It is obvious that Paul here refers to circumcision as an outward sign that separated the Jews from the gentiles – with outside distinction.

However in both Romans and Galatians, Paul expands on the idea of circumcision as an inward sign. For instance in the book of Romans, Paul teaches that circumcision is certainly of value to Jews, for it is the sign of their commitment to the law of God: "For circumcision indeed is of value if you obey the law" (Rom 2:25a). For Paul, people are circumcised if they obey the law, "but if you break the law, your circumcision becomes uncircumcision" (Rom 2:25b), or you are no better off than an uncircumcised gentile. On these passages, John Stott says that Paul

> does not deny the divine origin of circumcision, but he relativizes its value on the ground that he who is circumcised "is required to obey the whole law." For circumcision is the sign of covenant membership, and covenant membership demands obedience. . . . The ultimate sign, the *bona fide* evidence, of membership of the covenant of God is neither circumcision nor possession of the law, but the obedience which both circumcision and the law demand.[12]

For Paul, obedience to God's word is linked to true circumcision. If then people keep God's word, they are circumcised. Paul brought this argument to show that Jews have no ability to boast since any disobedience leads to uncircumcision even when one is outwardly circumcised. Paul seems to further the idea of circumcision of the heart, "For no one is a Jew who is merely one outwardly, nor is circumcision outward and physical. But a Jew is one inwardly, and circumcision is a matter of the heart, by the Spirit, not by the letter. His praise is not from man but from God" (Rom 2:28–29).

---

12. John Stott, *Romans: God's Good News for the World* (Downers Grove, IL: InterVarsity Press, 1994), 93.

In Romans, Paul seems to read through the Old Testament prophets including Moses, Jeremiah, and Ezekiel who taught that true circumcision is a matter of the heart (see, for example, Deut 30:6; Jer 4:4; 9:25; Ezek 44:6–9). But Paul takes it further by affirming that a faithful believer, though physically uncircumcised, is regarded by God as circumcised. Both Jews and gentiles are saved by grace, whether they are circumcised or not. They are both justified on the basis of their faith, apart from works of the law. In Romans 3:28–30, Paul writes, "For we hold that one is justified by faith apart from works of the law. Or is God the God of Jews only? Is he not the God of Gentiles also? Yes, of Gentiles also, since God is one – who will justify the circumcised by faith and the uncircumcised through faith."

Moving to Romans 4, Paul bases his arguments on Abraham by explaining that Abraham served as an example of a person whose faith was counted to him as righteousness: "For what does the Scripture say? 'Abraham believed God, and it was counted to him as righteousness'" (Rom 4:3). Paul argues that both gentiles and Jews are justified by faith because Abraham was counted righteous before he was circumcised.

In the Gospels, especially John, we see in Christ's argument on the Sabbath that circumcision supersedes the strictness of Sabbath (John 7:22–23). But in Romans 4:9–12, Paul shows that justification supersedes circumcision. Paul's argument is that Abraham did not receive circumcision in order to obtain righteousness, but as a sign or seal of the righteousness that he had by faith while he was still uncircumcised. Therefore, Abraham is the father of all who believe without being circumcised, as well as those who are circumcised but also follow the example of Abraham's faith.

In the book of Galatians, Paul seems to press the same arguments. For example in both Romans and Galatians, he quotes Genesis 15:6 "And [Abraham] believed the LORD, and he counted it to him as righteousness" (Rom 4:3; Gal 3:6). Paul wrote the book of Galatians to counter those who were teaching that Christians must be circumcised in order to be justified by God.

In Galatians 5:6, Paul argues, "For in Christ Jesus neither circumcision nor uncircumcision counts for anything, but only faith working through love." Paul starts this chapter by explaining how Christ has set us free from the demands of the law like circumcision. Paul's main appeal to the Galatians is that if they let themselves be circumcised, then Christ will be of no advantage. He reminds them that we are justified by grace on the grounds of our faith, not on works like circumcision. Paul concludes the book of Galatians with these words:

> It is those who want to make a good showing in the flesh who would force you to be circumcised, and only in order that they may not be persecuted for the cross of Christ. For even those who are circumcised do not themselves keep the law, but they desire to have you circumcised that they may boast in your flesh. But far be it from me to boast except in the cross of our Lord Jesus Christ, by which the world has been crucified to me, and I to the world. For neither circumcision counts for anything, nor uncircumcision, but a new creation. (Gal 6:12–15)

The epistles of Galatians and Romans reveal that physical circumcision, mentioned also in Ephesians, is in contrast with circumcision of the heart. Nevertheless, Paul found it necessary to remind the believing gentiles in Ephesus of their problem in the past, that they were "Gentiles in the flesh" (Eph 2:11). The question that may be raised is why should Paul remind them of this physical circumcision and not expound on the true circumcision of the heart?

Paul probably wanted the Gentiles to remember their former position so that they would truly grasp the reality of their new position in Christ. Harold Hoemer best explains in these words:

> Paul is using these descriptions only to make it vivid and to remind the Gentiles not to forget their past alienation from God and the great disparity between them and the Jews. Believing Gentiles now have the privilege to be united with believing Jews in one body. The Gentiles who were probably in the majority, could easily forget history and look with arrogance towards Jews. This is not unlike what Paul did in Rom 11:11–24 (esp. vv. 17–20).[13]

Strangers to the Covenants

God entered a covenant relationship first with Noah and his descendants (Gen 6:18; 9:9), then with Abraham and his descendants including Isaac, Jacob, and their descendants (Gen 15, 17; Lev 26:42). Later God made a covenant with the nation of Israel through Moses at Mount Sinai (Exod 19–20). Having entered into a covenant with the Israelites, God gave them the law found in the books of Exodus, Leviticus, and Deuteronomy. Their agreement to do all that the Lord had said was a sign of entering this covenant (Exod 19:5–8).

---

13. Harold W. Hoehner, *Ephesians: An Exegetical Commentary* (Grand Rapids: Baker Academic, 2002), 355.

By declaring "All that the LORD has spoken we will do" (19:8), the Israelites were bound to obey God's will as expressed in the Law of Moses. On his side, God promised the Israelites his almighty protection and blessings, but lawbreakers would face dreadful punishments. To these covenants God added another covenant with David and his descendants which was the promise of salvation through the Messiah (2 Sam 7; Isa 11). The apostle Paul says that "They are Israelites, and to them belong the adoption, the glory, the covenants, the giving of the law, the worship, and the promises. To them belong the patriarchs, and from their race, according to the flesh, is the Christ, who is God over all, blessed forever. Amen" (Rom 9:4–5).

Paul tells the gentiles to remember that they were "strangers to the covenants of promise" (Eph 2:12). They were hopeless as far as eternal salvation is concerned. They had no national hope in the rule of the promised Messiah. In other words, they didn't have any promised Messiah to deliver and to rule over them. They were also atheists, idolaters, or people without God. They did not know the true God, and they did not worship him as God. This is also true for Africans who neither know God nor worship him for who he is. Pre-Christian Africans were far removed from fellowship with God, lost in the deserts of sins.

We need to realize that our alienation from God is the root of all the problems Africa is facing today. Our countries have cried for peace, but it is nowhere to be found. Leaders have come and gone, but no one could give the peace we all long for. It is due to our state of being alienated from God that we see the strife increasing day after day. But Paul introduces us to a reality that makes our souls jump in excitement.

After describing the scope of sin and its terrible consequences in the first part of Ephesians 2, Paul moves to the marvelous reality of Christ's redemptive work. Paul wanted the gentiles to understand their former position with God before he moved to explain God's love manifested at the cross: "But now in Christ Jesus you who once were far off have been brought near by the blood of Christ" (Eph 2:13).

Christ Our Peace

Most African tribes or ethnic groups seem to be in a state of strife and enmity. It is infuriating when Christians within the church of Christ misinterpret the gospel in their relationships. Our marriages have been a battlefield of great disunity. It is so sad when we, the members of the church, think of one another only in terms of nationality, tribe, upbringing, etc. We are called into one body, and we must cease to think of others in terms of the things that divide us because Christ "is our peace, who has made us both one and has broken down in his flesh the dividing wall of hostility by abolishing the law of commandments expressed in ordinances" (Eph 2:14–15).

Paul explains in these verses that Christ is the one who gives us peace with God which then flows through us that we might have peace with others. Paul does this by drawing an analogy to the temple. During the time of Jesus, the temple area was divided in five sections. Inside the building was the Holy Place where the lampstand, incense altar, and table of bread were placed, and the Holy of Holies which was separated by a veil from the Holy Place and contained the ark of the covenant. Outside the building was a courtyard with the altar of sacrifice where only priests and male Israelites were allowed. Beyond this courtyard was another courtyard for Jewish women, and beyond the court of the women was the court of the gentiles, a

> large, lower, outer court . . . which surrounded the inner courts and was separated from them by a balustrade and a series of warning notices. Two of these have been excavated, written in Latin and Greek and forbidding trespass by Gentiles into the inner areas, on pain of death.[14]

These walls in the temple illustrate the hostility of the Jews toward the gentiles. Gentiles were considered as cast out people; Jews thought of them as unclean. Therefore, the gentiles were also hostile toward the Jews. An illustration can be drawn from the angry reaction of certain Jews who falsely accused Paul of defiling the temple by bringing Trophimus, a gentile, into the temple courtyard (Acts 21:27–30) where Gentiles were forbidden. Paul was surely thinking of this hostility when he wrote about it in the book of Ephesians (Eph 2:14–18).

Paul explains that Christ came to overthrow this wall that was separating the Jews from the gentiles. As a result, the gentiles have access to the Holy Place together with Jews. Christ came to do away with the old way of worship. Both Jews and gentiles now have free access to God because the separating wall has been demolished through Christ shedding his blood on the cross. The author of Hebrews says,

---

14. Philips W. Comfort and Walter A. Elwell, *Tyndale Bible Dictionary: A Comprehensive Guide to the People, Places, and Important Words of the Bible* (Carol Stream, IL: Tyndale House, 2001), 1246.

So Christ has now become the High Priest over all the good
things that have come. He has entered that greater, more perfect
Tabernacle in heaven, which was not made by human hands and is
not part of this created world. With his own blood – not the blood
of goats and calves – he entered the Most Holy Place once for all
time and secured our redemption forever. (Heb 9:11–12 NLT)

But how did Christ destroy this wall of hostility between the Jews and
gentiles? How did he demolish the wall so that both Jews and gentiles may have
access to the Most Holy Place through him? Paul explains that Christ abolished
"the dividing wall of hostility by abolishing the law of commandments
expressed in ordinances" (Eph 2:14–15). What is the law of commandments?
These are the Mosaic precepts contained in the book of Leviticus concerning
the priesthood. They are rules and regulations that guided the Israelites in
their ritual and sacrificial system of worship including burnt offerings, meal
offerings, peace offerings, sin offerings, guilt offerings, etc. But Christ abolished
this Mosaic sacrificial system. Hebrews 7:18–19 says, "Yes, the old requirement
about the priesthood was set aside because it was weak and useless. For the law
never made anything perfect. But now we have confidence in a better hope,
through which we draw near to God" (NLT).

The reason why Christ did away with this Mosaic system was first of all
"that he might create in himself one new man in place of the two, so making
peace" (Eph 2:15). Thomas Schreiner affirms that "both Jews and Gentiles
also need to be reconciled to God, and Paul locates their enmity to 'the law of
commandments and ordinances' (Eph 2:15), which likely refers to their failure
to keep God's law. Nor is the need for repentance limited to gentiles, for the
message of peace is also proclaimed to Jews, who are 'near' (Eph 2:17)."[15]

Through his death on the cross and his resurrection, Christ has brought
both Jews and gentiles into the same body. Through Christ, the church was
created where both Jews and gentiles are partakers of the same blessings in
him. The purpose was to bring people from different nationalities and from
different tribes into one organism, the church or the body of Christ.

We examined the church as the body of Christ in chapter two. The body
of Christ is used as a metaphor to illustrate the unity and the harmony that
should be found among its members. Paul writes, "For just as the body is
one and has many members, and all members of the body, though many, are
one body, so it is with Christ. For in one Spirit we were all baptized into one

---

15. Schreiner, *New Testament Theology*, 364.

body – Jews or gentiles, slaves or free – and all were made to drink of one Spirit" (1 Cor 12:12–13). At the day of our redemption, we were put in the body of Christ. We were not attached to the body, but we became the body of Christ who is the head.

As the body cannot function properly without a missing member, so it is true with the church of Christ. We are doing harm to the body of Christ when we encourage divisions in the church. For example, the church in Africa will not function properly when we allow tribalism to find its way into our intercultural marriages. And the reason we are still living this tragedy in Africa is because we have not fully experienced the peace that comes to us through salvation in Christ. Martyn Lloyd-Jones writes,

> We are called into one body . . . It is as I know I am in Christ, and look at another and know that he is in Christ, that I can forgive and forget, I can join hands and humble myself with him. We are all one in Christ, and we are going to spend our eternity in glory together. It is as we remember that, and only as we know that that is true of us, that there can be a true, a real, a lasting peace.[16]

The second reason why Christ abolished the Mosaic sacrificial system was to "reconcile us both to God in one body through the cross, thereby killing the hostility" (Eph 2:16). This verse brings us to the ultimate reason of Christ's sacrificial act on the cross. The section that started in alienation from God (2:11–12) ends in reconciliation in Christ by means of his death on the cross. Paul moves so systematically to show that our alienation from God is the cause of hostility. Because of this hostility between us and God, there is enmity between ourselves. All of our relationships will go wrong if our relationship with God is wrong in the first place.

But through Christ, we are drawn near to God. We have been reconciled back to God that we should be devoted to him. Through our reconciliation to God, Christ has killed the hostility that was between the Jews and gentiles by creating the church in which we are all one. In Christ we have peace and harmony with both God and with other members of the body of Christ. Now, we should not think of people only in terms of their nationality or tribe because we have all been reconciled to God.

The verb "to reconcile" leads to another idea that we should bear in mind. To reconcile is to bring back to a former state of harmony. When God created

---

16. Martyn Lloyd-Jones, *God's Way of Reconciliation: An Exposition of Ephesians Two* (Edinburgh: Banner of Truth, 1980), 282.

Adam and Eve, he put them in the garden and gave them dominion over all creatures. They lived in harmony with God and with one another before the fall. But as soon as their relationship with God went wrong, the two started to live in disharmony because of the infiltrated sin. Michael A. Grisanti puts it this way:

> Adam's sin disrupted the accomplishments of God's intentions for the creation (chap. 3). Adam and Eve's sin marred God's perfect order and initiated the human tendency to rebel against God's rule. No longer would the earth and animal world willingly submit to His direction. Adam's sin disrupted the harmony of all man's relationships (with God, with other human beings, with creation).[17]

But God, being gracious, promised a victory for the woman's offspring through conflict by telling the serpent, "I will put enmity between you and the woman, and between your offspring and her offspring; he shall bruise your head, and you shall bruise his heel" (Gen 3:15). Everybody born into the world is fallen and acts more like the devil than God (John 8:44). But God himself initiated the provision that would enable Adam and his offspring to return to harmony with God. There has been and will continue to be conflict between Adam's offspring, but by regeneration, we can find peace and harmony with each other (Rom 16:20; Gal 3:16). We see God's provision provided in Christ by mean of his redemptive work on the cross. Thomas Schreiner writes,

> Reconciliation means that friendship with God has been restored, so that the fellowship Adam enjoyed with God in the garden has been renewed and amplified. Reconciliation in Pauline theology is invariably dependent upon the cross of Christ. Paul emphasizes, therefore, the hostility of human beings toward God, so that the breach in their relationship with God must be repaired. Reconciliation is not only with God but also with one another. Jews and Gentiles are now united with one another through the cross of Christ.[18]

Christ's work of reconciliation has placed on us a biblical demand to exercise peace within the church. In our contacts with other people, peace

---

17. Michael A. Grisanti in Eugene H. Merrill, Mark F. Rooker, and Michael A. Grisanti, *The World and the Word: An Introduction to the Old Testament* (Nashville: B&H, 2011), 185.

18. Thomas Schreiner, *The King in His Beauty: A Biblical Theology of the Old and New Testaments* (Grand Rapids: Baker Academic, 2013), 557–58.

should be our goal because Christ has reconciled us back to God. Look at these verses for example: Romans 12:18: "If possible, so far as it depends on you, live peaceably with all." Romans 14:19: "So then let us pursue what makes for peace and for mutual upbuilding." Colossians 3:15: "And let the peace of Christ rule in your hearts, to which indeed you were called in one body. And be thankful."

Conclusion

Paul ends this section by explaining that Christ "came and preached peace to you who were far off and peace to those who were near" (Eph 2:17). Through the apostles' preaching, both gentiles and Jews have been reconciled to God by Christ. The message of the cross has reconciled the two alienated parties by incorporating them in the body of Christ. Gentiles are no longer alienated from God; they have been brought into the body of Christ through the gospel.

As the church in Africa, we are to faithfully preach Christ, the prince of peace. The problem of divisions in the church, the problem of tribalism, etc. can only be alleviated by people fully understanding the gospel. And I should emphasize here that prosperity gospel cannot do this. It is only through faithful preaching of the true gospel that people can be brought near to God. The gospel reveals how terrible our sins are. It shows us the depth of our deadness in sins. It perfectly describes our former condition of enmity and rebellion against God. It gives us knowledge of ourselves so that we may appreciate God's initiation of peace-making with us.

The greatest problem of Africa has always been the problem of peace. This problem has been so much manifested in our social interpretation of traditions related to church, marriages, tribalism, etc. The cure for this problem is having Bible-based local churches preach the word of God because the word of God is not only food for our hungry minds, it is also medicine for our diseased and troubled hearts where our strife and enmity reside. Pastors should also encourage their congregations with practical acts of love like the following:

- Have meals together in each other's house so as to experience the lives of different ethnic groups within our local churches.
- Encourage intertribal or intercultural marriages among believers in Christ.
- Promote multiethnic Bible study groups or plant multicultural churches across Africa.

- Share the African realities of suffering by extending and accepting invitations to experience the life of fellow Christians in their different situations.[19]
- Get to one another's cultures, for example, by living in one another's homes.
- Learn a different dialect represented in the church.
- Encourage regular fellowships of members.

However, while we may come up with practical steps to try to heal the problem of divisions, without a better understanding of the mystery of Christ, people will likely fall back into divisions. All attempts at peace-making are bound to fail among human beings unless they are based upon the reconciliation to God we have received in Christ.

---

19. Tokunboh Adeyemo and Emmanuel Ayee, *Following Jesus in a Segregational Society* (Nairobi, Kenya: AEAM, 1989), 35–36.

Conclusion

All through this book, I have sought to explain the mystery of the church, which is something that our finite mind cannot fully grasp, and discuss its implications in Africa in its multicultural state. We defined the mystery as the coming of Jews and gentiles to a complete equality in the new or gospel dispensation in Christ. However going through the Old Testament accounts on the gentiles, we realized that the mystery was not something entirely new. Thus in the first part of the book, we defined the church as a collection of God-glorifying saints, people from different ethnicities, tribes, and nations who have been called out of the world to belong to God and sent back to the world to witness about the gospel of Christ.

I also emphasized that when we come to Christ, we renounce every Christless thing, our sinful way of life, and our former religious allegiances in order to be united to Christ. We turn away from the worthless things of our religion and turn to the living God (Acts 14:15); we move from death to life (Eph 2:1–6); we move from darkness to light (2 Cor 4:4–6; Eph 5:8). Thus conversion to Christ necessitates a measure of cutting oneself off from a former way of living. It involves turning away from our "idols to serve the living and true God" (1 Thess 1:9). Anyone who belongs to Christ has become a new person. The old life is gone; a new life has begun (2 Cor 5:17). What then becomes the identity of African believers as the gospel is preached to them?

Our union to Christ does not imply a total denying of our cultural identity. The gospel is not only the power of God to free us from our sinful cultural practices but is also God's instrument to reshape the culture; it affirms and enriches some good elements found in the culture. For example, some traditional African ethics such as generosity, hospitality, community, etc. are also emphasized in the Bible to be developed in the Christian life. Concurrently, in the view of the gospel, some elements of any culture are definitely condemned and must be abolished.

Thus the goal of salvation is to unite people from diverse cultures into one organism, the body of Christ. The apostle Paul wrote to the Philippians, "Therefore God has highly exalted [Christ] and bestowed on him the name that is above every name, so that at the name of Jesus every knee should bow, in heaven and on earth and under the earth, and every tongue confess that

Jesus Christ is Lord, to the glory of God the Father" (Phil 2:9–11). This is what God is accomplishing in the church. Through the gospel, he is bringing people from diverse ethnic groups under the lordship of Christ for his own glory. Our allegiance is no longer to the traditional way of life, or to our idols, but to Christ Jesus who through the Holy Spirit has baptized different cultural people "into one body – Jews or Greeks, slaves or free – and all were made to drink of one Spirit" (1 Cor 12:13).

Thus the mystery of the church should not be equated with a cultural uniformity of its members but with equality and unity in diversity. This unity in cultural diversity finds its climactic expression in the new Jerusalem – "prepared as a bride adorned for her husband" (Rev 21:2) – which is characterized not by Jews only but by a glorified people from different tongues and nations who have been united to Christ (Rev 7:9–10; 21:22–27).

In the second part of this book, we tried to point out some defects in the African idea of Christ by examining the works of some prominent African theologians such as John Mbiti, Kwame Bediako, and Bolaji Idowu. We saw that it can be misleading to conclude that Christ came to complete an element that was missing in the primal religions in Africa, an idea that John Mbiti advocates. Had they taken into full account the negative features of primal African cultures in their writings, they would have shed even more light on the relationship between the continuity and discontinuity of the understanding of God in Africa, but unfortunately they do not seem to do this.

On the one hand, I agree with Kwame Bediako's assessment of the continuities and discontinuities between Africa's primal religions and Christianity, and it is definitely useful for correcting Western misrepresentations which equate pre-Christian African religions with animism. Bediako's purpose to shed positive light on Africa's prior understanding of God and its continuity with the gospel deserves some applause. However, I notice that an African assessment of the primal worldview would also reveal specific weaknesses. Byang Kato acknowledges that,

> While it is biblically and historically true that Africans as well as any other society of human beings know of God through general revelation, it is equally true that the traditional worship in Africa is the result of the total depravity that has set in (Romans 1:19–21). The traditional worshipper must be rescued from dumb idols to serve the Living God (1 Thessalonians 1:9).[1]

---

1. Byang H. Kato, *Theological Pitfalls in Africa* (Kisumu, Kenya: Evangel, 1975), 163.

On the other hand, however, the conclusion that Christ does not negate African traditional religions but crowns them is inconsistent with the Scriptures. Primal African traditional religious people, like people practicing any other religion, need Christ who has borne the wrath of God that is against all unrighteousness (Rom 1:18). God's wrath and curse was directed against Christ so that all elect Africans who once were far off might be brought near by the blood of Christ (Eph 2:13).

Bibliography

Adeyemo, Tokunboh, and Emmanuel Ayee. *Following Jesus in a Segregational Society.* Nairobi, Kenya: AEAM, 1989.

Allis, Oswald T. *Prophecy and the Church.* Phillipsburg, NJ: P&R Publishing, 1974.

Barrett, C. K. *The Gospel According to John: An Introduction with Commentary and Notes on the Greek Text.* London: SPCK, 1955.

Beale, G. K. *The Temple and the Church's Mission: A Biblical Theology of the Dwelling Place of God.* NSBT 17. Downers Grove, IL: InterVarsity Press, 2004.

Beale, G. K., and Benjamin L. Gladd. *Hidden but Now Revealed: A Biblical Theology of Mystery.* Downers Grove, IL: InterVarsity Press, 2014.

Bediako, Kwame. *Jesus in Africa: The Christian Gospel in African History and Experience.* Akropong-Akuapem, Ghana: Regnum Africa, 2000 (in association with Paternoster).

———. *Theology and Identity: The Impact of Culture upon Christian Thought in the Second Century and in Modern Africa.* Oxford: Regnum, 1999.

Bruce, F. F. *The Book of the Acts: The New International Commentary of the New Testament,* revised edition. Grand Rapids: Eerdmans, 1988.

Calvin, John. *Institutes of the Christian Religion.* Translated from the first French edition of 1541 by Robert White. Edinburgh: Banner of Truth, 2014.

Campbell, Constantine R. *Paul and Union with Christ: An Exegetical and Theological Study.* Grand Rapids: Zondervan, 2012.

Carson, D. A. *The Gagging of God: Christianity Confronts Pluralism.* Grand Rapids: Zondervan, 1996.

Comfort, Philip W., and Walter A. Elwell. *The Tyndale Bible Dictionary: A Comprehensive Guide to the People, Places, and Important Words of the Bible.* Carol Stream, IL: Tyndale, 2001.

Elliott, Mark W., ed. *Old Testament XI – Isaiah 40-66: Ancient Christian Commentary on Scripture.* Downers Grove, IL: InterVarsity Press, 2007.

Enns, Paul. *The Moody Handbook of Theology,* revised edition. Chicago: Moody, 2008.

Erickson, Millard J. *Christian Theology.* Grand Rapids, MI: Baker Academic, 2013.

Feinberg, John S. *Continuity and Discontinuity: Perspectives on the Relationship between the Old and New Testaments.* Wheaton, IL: Crossway, 1988.

Feldman, Louis H. *Judaism and Hellenism Reconsidered.* Boston: Brill Academic, 2006.

Gehman, Richard J. *African Traditional Religion in Biblical Perspective – Revised Edition.* Nairobi: East African Educational Publishers, 2005.

Goldstein, Joshua S., and Jon C. Pevehouse. *International Relations: Brief Fourth Edition.* New York: Pearson Longman, 2008.

Hendriksen, William. *Galatians and Ephesians: New Testament Commentary.* Edinburgh: Banner of Truth, 1968.

———. *Matthew: New Testament Commentary.* Edinburgh: Banner of Truth, 1974.

Hoehner, Harold W. *Ephesians: An Exegetical Commentary.* Grand Rapids: Baker Academic, 2002.

Idowu, E. Bolaji. "Faiths in Interaction." *Orita: Ibadan Journal of Religious Studies* 4, no. 2 (Dec 1970): 85–102.

———. "The Study of Religion, with Special Reference to African Traditional Religion." *Orita: Ibadan Journal of Religious Studies* 1, no. 1 (Jun 1957): 3–12.

Kaiser, Jr., Walter C. *The Promise-Plan of God: A Biblical Theology of the Old and New Testaments.* Grand Rapids: Zondervan, 2008.

Kato, Byang H. *Theological Pitfalls in Africa.* Kisumu, Kenya: Evangel, 1975.

Lewis, C. S. "Christian Apologetics." [1945] In *God in the Dock: Essays on Theology and Ethics.* Grand Rapids: Eerdmans, 1970.

Lloyd-Jones, Martyn. *God's Way of Reconciliation: An Exposition of Ephesians Two.* Edinburgh: Banner of Truth, 1980.

———. *Romans, Exposition of Chapter 1: The Gospel of God.* Edinburgh: Banner of Truth, 1985.

Magezi, Christopher, and Jacob T. Igba. "African Theology and African Christology: Difficulty and Complexity in Contemporary Definitions and Methodological Frameworks." *Theological Studies* 74, no. 1 (2018). https://hts.org.za/index.php/hts/article/view/4590.

Mbiti, John S. *African Religions and Philosophy.* Nairobi: Heinemann Kenya, 1969.

———. *Concepts of God in Africa.* London: SPCK, 1970.

———. *The Crisis of Mission in Africa.* Mukono: Uganda Church Press, 1971.

McGrath, Alister. *Christian Belief for Everyone: Book One: Faith and the Creeds.* London: SPCK, 2013.

———. *Christian Theology: An Introduction,* 6th edition. Chichester: John Wiley, 2017.

———. *The Living God: Christian Belief for Everyone.* London: SPCK, 2013.

McKnight, Scot, and Grant R. Osborne. *The Face of New Testament Studies: A Survey of Recent Research.* Grand Rapids: Baker Academic, 2004.

Merrill, Eugene H., Mark F. Rooker, and Michael A. Grisanti. *The World and the Word: An Introduction to the Old Testament.* Nashville: B&H, 2011.

Murray, John. *Collected Writings of John Murray: Volume One – The Claims of Truth.* Edinburgh: Banner of Truth, 1976.

Rousseau, Jean-Jacques. *Social Contract and Discourses.* Translated by G. D. H. Cole. Hawthorne, CA: BN Publishing, 2007.

Russell, Bertrand. *Unpopular Essays.* London: Unwin Brothers, 1921.

Schreiner, Thomas. *The King in His Beauty: A Biblical Theology of the Old and New Testaments.* Grand Rapids: Baker Academic, 2013.

———. *New Testament Theology: Magnifying God in Christ.* Grand Rapids: Baker Academic, 2008.

Sproul, R. C. *Truths We Confess: Volume Two – Salvation and the Christian Life.* Phillipsburg, NJ: P&R, 2007.

Stanton, Graham N., and Guy G. Stroumsa, eds. *Tolerance and Intolerance in Early Judaism and Christianity.* Cambridge: Cambridge University Press, 1998.

Stott, John R. W. *Romans: God's Good News for the World.* Downers Grove, IL: InterVarsity Press, 1994.

Strange, Daniel. *Their Rock Is Not Like Our Rock: A Theology of Religions.* Grand Rapids: Zondervan Academic, 2015.

Tarsus, David Kirwa. *A Different Way of Being: Towards a Reformed Theology of Ethnopolitical Cohesion for the Kenyan Context.* Carlisle, UK: Langham Monographs, 2019.

Thiselton, Anthony C. *The First Epistle to the Corinthians: The New International Greek Testament Commentary.* Grand Rapids: Eerdmans, 2000.

Tozer, A. W. *The Knowledge of the Holy: The Attributes of God, Their Meaning in the Christian Life.* San Francisco: Harper Collins, 1961.